THE BOOK OF
LAZ

CHRIS IACHETTA

ARCHWAY
PUBLISHING

Archway Publishing books may be ordered through booksellers or by contacting:

Archway Publishing
1663 Liberty Drive
Bloomington, IN 47403
www.archwaypublishing.com
844-669-3957

ISBN: 978-1-4808-9834-9 (sc)
ISBN: 978-1-4808-9832-5 (hc)
ISBN: 978-1-4808-9833-2 (e)

Library of Congress Control Number: 2020920968

Print information available on the last page.

Archway Publishing rev. date: 11/13/2020

Dedication

THIS IS DEDICATED TO EVERYONE WHO DOUBTED ME. THE FOSTER parents who didn't want me. The teachers who said I wouldn't make it. The group home staff, who thought I'd end up in jail or dead. My adoptive mom, who said I would amount to nothing. Anyone who has ever called me a deadbeat or a loser—this one's for you.

More importantly, I'd like to dedicate this book to my wife, without whom I wouldn't be here today. None of this would be possible without her.

Contents

Acknowledgments

I'D LIKE TO THANK MICHAEL JORDAN, KOBE BRYANT, AND THE NBA, for being my inspirations and getting me through the awful shit I have written about in this book.

Introduction

I STILL DON'T UNDERSTAND WHY GOD WOULD WANT SOMEBODY TO go through the shit I went through. I mean, seriously, what's with this chick? All I know is I'm blessed to be alive. I wasn't sure I'd make it, but here I am.

I have tried to be as authentic as possible in this book. If you're in this book, you might remember some of these events differently. That's okay. I'm just telling my story the way I remember it. I'm sitting in my two-bedroom apartment, quarantined during the coronavirus pandemic, with nothing to do and a story to tell.

If you're going through some tough times, I hope this book helps you realize you are not alone. And you can make it through anything. You just have to hang in there a little bit longer. Please don't give up.

TRIGGER WARNING: My story can be heavy. This book deals with sexual abuse, depression, suicidal thoughts, physical abuse, emotional abuse, and extreme anger, among other things. If you or someone you know is struggling, here are some resources that can help:

- Suicide Prevention Hotline: 800-273-8255
- Crisis Hotline: 800-854-7771
- Crisis Text Line: text HOME to 741741
- National Domestic Violence Hotline: 800-799-7233

1

Lazarus

I was named Lazarus when I was born. My mom, Gina, was cracked out as all hell when she had me and my siblings. I'm the second of four kids. Paula is the oldest, then me, then Kate, then Mikey. My siblings have fairly normal names—Paula, Kate, Mikey—but I got stuck with Lazarus. What in the world was Gina thinking?

The only way I can think to explain it is with the story of Lazarus from the Bible. That's the only thing that makes sense to me. Lazarus was an average guy, but he died, and Jesus raised him from the dead. He had a life-changing experience, and people wanted to hear his story. They wanted to know about his death and how he had been brought back to life. The name Lazarus means "God has helped"—*has helped* already. His parents named him that before the miracle had even happened. Is that why I was named Lazarus? I was going to go through some life-changing shit, and God was going to help me through it?

A person who was as drugged out as my mom could not have been in her right mind when she had me. She must have been on cocaine, speed, hash, and all sorts of other stuff. Definitely coke. There's no way that devil came up with the name Lazarus on her own. She never read a Bible. Get the hell outta here. Most normal people open the Bible and are like "Okay, here are some good names: Josh, Paul, Peter, John …" But not Lazarus. No one is named Lazarus. It sounds crazy, but I just know the name Lazarus was put into her head by someone (or something) who knew what was going to happen to me. I was going to come close to death multiple times and rise every time. Lazarus was the only name that made sense for someone who was going to make it through hell like I did.

2

Gina

I NEVER MET MY DAD. I SAW A PHOTO OF HIM ONCE, BUT THAT WAS it. I can't remember what he looked like. Gina, on the other hand, I remember perfectly. I can't forget Gina. She was like five feet three, maybe 180 pounds, with blonde hair and wide shoulders. She was scary. She looked like the devil. And she was the devil. She made me eat my own puke. She almost killed me. She made me stand in the corner for a whole day with nothing but Tootsie Rolls to eat. She and her boyfriend did awful things to me and my sisters. She put me through so much shit. I wish she were still alive so I could ask her about it—not that she'd remember. She was so high and cracked out all the time, her brain must have been fried.

Gina lived in a dilapidated old building. Our house was part of a six- or seven-unit complex. Gina's mother, my grandma, lived next door to us. She was a weird-looking old lady with no teeth who wore a lot of muumuus. We weren't close. I didn't really know her. Gina's brother lived in another unit. We weren't close either. And there was some weird old man in one of the other units. He had these big-ass shoes that I was enamored with and glasses. He was useless. He just had big shoes. That's all I remember. There was a communal porch that stretched the whole width of the building. It was white and falling apart. It was a miracle the thing was still standing. It was barely hanging on. The whole structure we lived in should've been demolished. That's how bad it was. And there were bugs and roaches everywhere—huge roaches, the size of you and me.

My siblings and I were abused so much in that house. Gina beat us, then threatened us to make sure we wouldn't tell anyone. She always told us that if we said anything, she would hurt us. And she meant it. She would do it. Anytime we came home, we got hit—right in the face or in the back of the head. Sometimes with an open palm, sometimes with a fist. Sometimes she'd hit us with her belt, or any object she could find nearby. It didn't matter. She just wanted us to feel pain. I still don't know why.

I lived with Gina for only four years, but it felt like a lifetime. There were a lot of incidents at Gina's. For example, there was the fire incident. She put toast in the toaster, left something by the toaster, and then walked outside of the house. Back then, toasters weren't advanced like they are now. They were naturally fire hazards because they were so poorly designed. You could put anything near one, and it would light on fire. That moron left a newspaper next to ours, and all of a sudden, the kitchen was on fire. I came out of my bedroom and saw the counter on fire and didn't know what to do. I was confused. I'd never seen fire. I just kind of stared at it for a while. I didn't know what it was. It started as a small fire, but I watched it grow until it had burned most of the kitchen down.

Something eventually told me to get out. Something told me to walk out and yell, "Fire!" Gina was on the porch with her buddies, doing drugs. She was mad that I had interrupted them or something. I didn't know what else to do. I had never seen fire before. I hadn't put the toast in the toaster and walked away. But of course, Gina made it my fault. She went inside and called for help. They put the fire out, then she fucking beat me. She tried to blame me for starting the fire. Gina hit me so hard, for something I didn't even do. She did that a lot—just socked me in the mouth every time she got mad about something. That stupid toaster fire was her mistake, not mine.

It was the same with the steak. It was a typical night. Gina made steak and Spanish rice for dinner—that rice in the yellow box, the Goya kind you get at the store. The rice was fine, but she cooked the steak so badly that I think most dogs would've turned it down. Most raccoons probably would've turned it down. Street rats in the New York subways would've turned it down. That's how bad it was. I swear she put a whole container of salt on it. So much salt. I hated it. I mean, what did she expect me to do? I was four years old. Fuck. I tried it, and it was the worst-tasting thing. I still remember how bad it was. I didn't want to eat it. I would rather have starved. Gina didn't like that. She told me, "You can't leave until you finish everything on your plate." I fucking hated that rule. Any parent who tells their kid that—why don't you finish the lousy food and get back to me? Learn how to cook, and maybe your kid will eat the food. Morons. I put the steak in my mouth and shoved it in the back corner where she couldn't see it. She asked, "Did you eat everything like I told you to?" Obviously, I said yes. She didn't believe me, so she checked my mouth. She couldn't see the steak. Success! Or so I thought.

I went to the living room to find a place to get that damn steak out of my mouth and hide it. I looked around and noticed the two inches between the couch and the wall. Of course, Gina couldn't think to push the couch up to the wall like a normal person. She lived like a mutant. I climbed up onto the couch, leaned over the back, and spit. The steak fell out of my mouth to the floor. She must've seen me. A few minutes later, I was in the kitchen getting water, and she came in with the steak I had just spit behind the couch. She was holding it in her hand. It was covered in dirt and dust. Gina looked at me and snapped, "What the fuck is this?" and she slapped me right on the cheek. Nailed me. Good one, right in the head. I can still feel her handprint. My face was hot. I started to cry. It hurt so bad. *Bam!* She hit me again.

"What the fuck is this? Fucking eat it!" she yelled, and she smacked me again. I was crying. I was upset. I didn't want to eat it. She smacked me again. It was painful. I was so little, but she kept beating me up, all because I didn't want her stupid steak. After a few minutes of yelling and hitting, I ended up eating the steak with all the dust on it. It was filthy. You think that bitch could ever clean her place? Hell no. She could've been on an episode of *Hoarding: Buried Alive*. She fucking made me eat the dirty, dusty steak I'd spit out onto the floor. I just remember her hitting me in the face over and over and over again. I still don't get it. Why was she so mad at me? I didn't like the steak because she'd put salt on it. She was out here ready to kill me because her food sucked. I hadn't told her to be a bad chef. I'm pretty sure the recipe didn't call for a pound of salt. Almost thirty years later, I found out that Gina had died from choking on a piece of steak. If that's not poetic justice, I don't know what is. God has a twisted sense of humor, that's for sure.

There was also the rock incident. Gina, my siblings, and I were at the bus stop for some reason. I think Gina had an appointment. She didn't have a car, so we took the bus everywhere. Every time Gina looked away, I picked up a rock and threw it. I was trying to hit anything I could. I don't know why, but I loved the sound a rock made when it hit something. Right as Gina turned her head back toward me, I threw a rock at a car. I think it shattered the window. The driver was in the car, and he was pissed—and understandably so. I'd be mad if someone did that to my car too. But Gina was beyond mad. She threw me onto the ground and beat me, in the middle of the fucking sidewalk. When we got home, she beat me again. It just didn't stop. She beat me within an inch of my life. I just got hit all the fucking time. If I wasn't getting hit, I was getting yelled at. Or she was trying to drown me. It was just one fucked-up thing after another with Gina.

Sometimes my sisters and I would go days without eating. There just wasn't food in the house. Gina couldn't afford it. And she would leave us on our own for long periods of time. When you're a young kid, you don't really have a sense of time. You don't know if it's been days, weeks, or months. All I know is it felt like forever. We were constantly left on our own with no food or any way of taking care of ourselves. It was always scary when Gina left, because we didn't know how long she'd be gone. We needed our mom. We had no protection. The lights were off. I don't even know if we had locks on the doors. We would sit up in bed all night, watching the door, to make sure someone didn't come in.

We couldn't reach the kitchen sink, so when Gina left us alone, we had to drink water out of the toilet. We were smart enough to get a container of water. We knew water went in a container. But we couldn't reach the sink or cabinets, and I didn't think to use a stool or stand on a chair. I was too young to put two and two together. That thought didn't even cross my mind. One night, my older sister Paula needed water, and we were too scared to leave our bedroom. We were scared that Big Mike might be out there waiting for us. To get out of bed at all was difficult back then. We thought it was the most dangerous thing we could do. Getting up out of bed in the middle of the night? Are you stupid? That's how the boogeyman gets you. But Paula was thirsty. And my job was to protect my sisters at all costs. My job was to make sure they were okay. I don't know where I got that mindset from. But I did what I could. I grabbed a pitcher off the only counter I could reach and dipped it into the toilet to get Paula water to drink. Well, before that, I made the mistake of thinking vinegar was water. Idiot. How did I not know the difference? That's how hard I was on myself. Even now when I make a mistake, I don't forgive myself for it—because of what I went through then. We couldn't afford to make mistakes. If Paula was choking and couldn't drink water, we would be in big trouble. We might get hit or hurt. We might not make it. That was our reality. You might not make it if you made Gina mad enough. Had we stayed in that house, there's no way we would've made it. I wouldn't be here.

I think that's why Gina was hidden from me when I was an adult. If I had found her, I would've fucking beaten her like a piñata. I would've headbutted her mouth so fast. She would've gotten fuckin' yoked. I would've crushed her head. I'm sorry. I know that's bad. But she put me through hell—she and Big Mike.

3

Big Mike

BIG MIKE WAS GINA'S ... BOYFRIEND? PIMP? DRUG DEALER? ALL OF the above? I'm not sure. Maybe not her pimp. She was pretty ugly. Big Mike was an average-looking dude. He had blonde curly hair and a mustache but no beard. I remember he wore light wash jeans and a T-shirt. He sexually abused my sisters and me on a consistent basis for years. Gina was in on it too. She knew what was going on but was too high to do anything about it. One time we went to the living room to tell her about it, but she didn't care. She just shrugged us off or told us to get over it. Mom of the year right there.

Big Mike would come into the house, sometimes when Gina wasn't even there, and walk straight into whatever room my sisters and I were in. The worst room was the one in the back of the house, right near the cellar door. When you're a kid, you think basements are haunted. The boogeyman was in the basement waiting for you. Big Mike and my mom told us that all the time. "The boogeyman is gonna get you at night," they'd say. I used to lie awake at night, facing the door, waiting for it to happen. I was convinced the boogeyman was going to come in and get me and my sisters. Turns out there was a boogeyman. It was Big Mike.

He would walk into the house, head straight back to the bedroom, grab my sisters, and throw them onto the bed. Once he had them pinned, he would put his hand under their dresses, pull their underwear down, and touch their privates. Same drill every time. They cried and screamed and tried to get away, but Big Mike didn't care. I think he liked the struggle. Sick fuck. He assaulted them a lot. It wasn't a one-time thing. I see these stories in the news now, and I get it. I understand your pain. I can't even tell you how many times it happened to us. We lost track. It happened for years. We tried to fight him off, but we couldn't. He was big. We were little. I would try to fight him, and I'd lose, but I'd keep going. I would go at him with everything I had. I would kick him and smack him and scream. I would flail around, trying my hardest to get away and fend him off of me and my sisters, but I couldn't do it. Imagine someone two or three times your size grabbing you, pinning you down, and touching you in the most private, intimate places while you fight for your life to get free. It was horrifying. Big Mike and Gina often had to put me in another room so he could be alone with my sisters without having to worry about me trying to fight them off. Sometimes they'd put me in the cellar and lock the door. I was terrified. I was worried about getting kidnapped or killed by the boogeyman. I wanted to protect my sisters so badly, but I couldn't do anything from the basement. I felt helpless. I just had to sit there, afraid of the boogeyman, listening to my sisters scream and cry while Big Mike grunted and yelled at them to shut up. Sometimes Gina joined Big Mike when he molested my sisters. She never touched me, but she abused the girls. I can still hear my sisters' screams. That sound haunts me to this day.

When he was finished molesting the girls, Big Mike would molest me too. The worst memories I have are from the top bunk of our bunk bed. Big Mike climbed up into the bunk bed with me and held me down. I tried to get free, but he was too powerful. I wasn't strong enough to fight him off. He held me down with one hand, and with his other hand, he unzipped my pants and played with my dick. It was never just a quick touch, either. It felt like it lasted forever. I was so scared. I was trapped. Big Mike molested me several times—at least double digits. But he got my sisters more, a lot more. It happened so many times. It's the most horrifying thing when someone pulls down your pants and … you know. Or maybe you don't know. You're lucky if you don't. It has affected me to this day. My sex life was atrocious well into my adult life because I was dealing with this. Anytime I started to get physical with a girl, I'd have flashbacks to Big Mike stroking my dick. I was afraid of physical touch for years because of it. And I still feel like it's all my fault. For some reason I came to believe that all of this was my fault. I thought I wasn't good enough, or I deserved the bad things that happened to me for some reason. I thought I had done something in another life that caused me to have all this. Big Mike sexually abused me and my sisters, and I thought I deserved it. That shit sticks with you the rest of your life.

4

Christmas

WE THOUGHT WE WERE GOING TO HAVE A GOOD CHRISTMAS. THE gifts were great. We used to get gifts from the state because my mom couldn't afford to give us presents. She didn't have a job most of the time. When she did have a job, most of her money went to drugs. The rest of her money went to Big Mike. Big Mike had Timberlands—nice-looking work boots. And I was enamored with the boots. I thought, *Oh man, it would be cool to have some work boots.* I thought people looked cool and tough in them. I wanted to look cool and tough too. I wanted to match Big Mike. As much as he fucked with me and my sisters, he was the only male figure I had in my life at that point. I never knew my dad. I only knew Big Mike. So there was a part of me that wanted to be like him, despite everything he put us through. It's fucked-up, I know.

I got my work boots for Christmas. I got GI Joes and work boots and all sorts of cool stuff. Paula got a Barbie car. I don't remember what Kate got. I'm sure it was something cool. I think my baby brother Mikey was there. It was a great Christmas morning. Everyone was in a good mood. We felt like a real family. I was so excited to get my work boots and look like Big Mike. I was so happy that morning. Then Gina turned to me and my sisters and said,

"Take off your clothes, but leave your shoes on. We're going to take a picture by the tree."

We were confused. We were just little kids, but we knew that wasn't right. We were thinking, *What? That's not normal. You don't take your clothes off and stand in front of a tree with no clothes on.* We had been taught not to do things like that. That was the kind of thing we'd get in trouble for normally. And here she was, saying we had to do it. We knew that if we resisted, we would get beaten. No one wants to get beaten on Christmas. So we did what Gina asked. We got naked and stood in front of the Christmas tree. We took our shoes and clothes off, then put our shoes back on and stood in front of the tree. I wanted to play with my new toys and spend time with my sisters and have a good Christmas Day. But I'll be damned, that son of a bitch Gina took photos of us buck naked on Christmas Day in front of the tree, wearing nothing but our shoes. Wow, talk about humiliating. I had just come off the biggest high and was experiencing the lowest low. That was the type of shit that happened every day at Gina's. I can remember only a certain number of events because I was four. But if that's the kind of stuff I can remember, imagine what else was going on. I was getting my ass beaten every day. I had wanted work boots, and I got them, but I had to take naked pictures to pay for them. Nothing came for free with Gina. Everything had a price.

She made us take pictures naked on Christmas. It was the weirdest thing ever. The photo is somewhere in my file still. Some sick fuck still has that photo. Who takes pictures of a kid naked on Christmas?

5

The Bunk Bed

ONE OF THE WORST BEATINGS I GOT WAS WHEN MY SISTERS AND I broke the bunk bed. Gina smacked me three ways to Sunday for breaking that damn thing. That was fun. We were sleeping in the side room, right off the kitchen. It was a weird room. The bunk beds were on the right, and there was a door to the basement on the left. Gina had the room in the back. We were kids, so we liked to climb and jump on the bunk beds. We were in there jumping around on the top bunk, doing what kids do, having fun. And lo and behold, that shit snapped, and *BOOM*! I mean, it was a loud bang. We were okay—safe, not injured, just scared. We were nervous about what we knew was going to happen next.

We went out to the living room, and Gina immediately yelled at us. "What the fuck happened? What was that fucking noise?"

We wanted to lie, but we knew she would find out. So we told her: we broke the bunk bed. But instead of telling her my sisters did it, I said I did it. I took the blame for the whole thing. I was always trying to protect them. Gina got up from the couch and smacked me across the back. Then she hit me in the head. She hit me over and over and over again. She fucking beat my ass. She made me stand in the corner for a whole day as a punishment. She didn't let me have water or food. The only thing she let me eat was Tootsie Rolls. I still can't eat Tootsie Rolls because of it. That's all I had to eat. I had to face the wall and eat Tootsie Rolls while she yelled at me all day. She yelled things like "Think about what you did" and "You're retarded." I had to stand in the corner the next day too. More hitting, more insults, more Tootsie Rolls. It was awful. I was miserable. I got it—I'd broken the bunk bed. I knew it wasn't really me who had done it—it was my sisters—but I didn't want them to get hit. With the sexual abuse and everything else we went through, I just knew I had to do whatever I could to protect them. All I wanted was for them to be safe. It's the same even now. For a while my sister was getting beaten by some big cocksucker who roided out and went to the gym. And it killed me that I wasn't in the same city to protect her. I just want them both to be okay. I took a lot of ass whuppings for them, even for things that weren't my fault. I think Gina liked beating me. It didn't matter why. She just hated me. She even said it later on. She fucking hated me. I couldn't do anything right. A few years later, some of my foster parents read my file and told me that Gina had wanted my sisters to go home with her, but not me. Not the boy. I guess that's why she tried to kill me.

6

The Bathtub

I REMEMBER SITTING IN THE BATHTUB, PLAYING WITH MY TOYS. IT was a normal day—some good moments, some bad. I'd had fun with my sisters, but I'd also gotten beaten and screamed at in the kitchen. I got yelled at and hit for everything. I got beaten all the time. That was a typical day. I got my ass beaten, I got screamed at, Gina got tired, we all chilled in the living room like one big happy family, and somehow, we survived to see another day.

We didn't take many baths. We didn't know any better. Gina was abusing drugs my entire childhood. She never thought about things like bathing her kids on a regular basis. But that day, she was sitting next to the tub, against the yellow wall of the bathroom. I had my little green rowboat and another toy in the water. I don't know where Kate was. Paula was in the kitchen nearby, looking into the bathroom. I could see her from the bathtub.

How the house worked was you walked into the living room, and straight ahead from the front door was the TV, an old TV with bunny ears. Then to your right there was a small hallway that led through to the kitchen. So when you walked in, if you turned right, you could see the kitchen. The couch was up against the wall by the hallway. When you walked straight to the kitchen, the bathroom was off to the right. And when you walked into the bathroom, the tub was right there on the right-hand side. The toilet was behind the tub. Weird layout.

I was sitting in the tub, playing with my toys, doing what kids do. Gina was just sitting there with a blank expression on her face—no emotion, just sitting there. I didn't notice anything out of the ordinary. She wasn't really engaged with me. Typical loser. Completely zoned out, like a moron. She was there, but she wasn't. She was empty. Then it started to change. She started to get into it with Paula. That's when I started to get concerned. She yelled at Paula, "If you fucking say anything, I'll fucking kill him!" She said it over and over again, then grabbed me by the head and shoved me underneath the water. She held me down for what felt like forever. I can't even describe how long it felt. I was panicking because her weight was completely on me. I was only four years old, so I was, I don't know, thirty-four to forty pounds? My head slammed against the bottom of the tub. I didn't know what was happening. The tub was over half full. I was really in it. I came back up, choking and trying to breathe, and she yelled at Paula again. "I'll kill him! I'll fucking kill him! I swear if you say anything, I'll kill him!"

That's when it got real. She grabbed my head again and slammed it back down. This time I was down for a while. I remember panicking. I remember the water coming in my mouth. And I was thrashing so hard. I remember bubbles. The yellow wallpaper. Gina's face. Paula crying. I was trying to close my mouth so the water wouldn't get in. I was scared, so scared. I was trying anything I could to get up, and I couldn't do it. I couldn't get up. She was so mad. I don't know why. She just wouldn't let me up. Then something happened. She must've been 175 to 200 pounds, and I was just a small kid. But somehow, I got up. I still don't know how. But I have some theories. Something pushed me up. I think somebody or something helped me. Somebody was looking out for me. The physics of it just didn't make sense. Someone my size versus someone her size? She wasn't a string bean. She had slammed me down so hard that my face smashed off the tub. That I wasn't knocked unconscious is crazy on its own. But okay, maybe she didn't hit me at the right angle, or I got lucky. Whatever. But she was on top of me for a long fucking time. And the only thing I kept thinking was "I have to get up, I have to get up, I have to get up." Something lifted me up that day. That's the only explanation. It had to be an angel or something. Whatever it was, it got me out of the water. Gina left the bathroom. Paula was crying and came over to check on me. I was lost. I was lost from that moment on.

After the bathtub, I really don't remember much. It's all a blur. That was when I hated my life for the first time. I just sat there in the tub, absolutely defeated—terrified, sobbing. Gina went to her room. I don't think I saw her the rest of the day. I think the police came around a week after that. Then it was over.

7

The Last Day

I REMEMBER THE LAST DAY WE WERE WITH GINA LIKE IT WAS YES-terday. It was a good day. Man, oh man, one of the best days. My sisters, my brother, and I were all in the living room, playing with our toys. I want to say it was spring. It seemed like it was decent weather out. We were playing, goofing off, doing what we normally did. Gina was watching TV and being lazy, like always, sitting on the same couch she had made me eat my own puke off of one day. If you've ever eaten your vomit, you know it's the worst taste in the world.

Anyway, I was sitting on the floor, playing with my GI Joes. Paula had her Barbies, and Kate was sitting in a high chair or some kind of children's chair over by Gina, who was seated on the farthest side of the couch toward the wall. Mikey was still a baby, so he was just sitting there. I was playing about two feet from the front door, which opened right into the living room. And Gina was just zoned out. She looked happy, though. People always look happiest when shit's about to go down. It's insane. People usually have the best looks on their faces before tragedy strikes. We had no idea what was about to happen. We had no idea our lives were about to be fucked up forever.

We heard a knock at the door. We aren't expecting anybody.

We didn't get visitors. They knocked again, louder the second time, and said, "Police! Police! Open the door!" They said it twice before they busted the door open. They kicked that bitch, and it flew open. They didn't fuck around with issues related to kids. When you fucked with kids, the cops would bring everything they had. They'd brought the cavalry that day. They had to have seven cars. That was insane back then—seven cars. They had everybody. They stormed in and yelled, "Don't fucking move!" and looked right at Gina. I didn't see if they had weapons. I think they did, but I didn't see because as soon as they busted in, I ran straight for the bedroom to get my work boots. I wasn't sure what was happening, but I knew I had to go get my work boots. I loved those boots. I almost got them too. I was so close. I got to the room, right off to the left of the kitchen, and couldn't find them. I couldn't find my boots because Paula hadn't picked up her fucking toys. She never picked up after herself. Although it was fairly neat that day, it was still messy enough that I couldn't find my work boots. They were always in my room, and they weren't there. I was so confused. I remember seeing Paula's Barbie car. For some reason I thought my boots might be under the car. I went to look under the car, and that's when an officer grabbed me.

Next thing I knew, I was outside. My sisters and I were put in the police car. I was in the middle, with my sisters on either side of me. I don't know where baby Mikey was. They must've had him in another car or something. We didn't see Gina. They must've had her against the wall. They weren't playing with her. With us, the officers were sweet and professional. They tried their hardest to make us feel safe and like everything was fine. But we heard the police yelling at Gina outside the car. "Don't fucking move! Don't move an inch!" That's what I remember them saying. Looking back, I wish they would've shot her that day. She was a quitter.

My sisters and I weren't really sure what was happening. We were confused. Where were we going? Who were these people? Why couldn't we stay at our house? What about my work boots? Why couldn't we be with our mom? Where was our brother? And we were sad. We had been having such a great day up until that point. I mean, I was four years old. I didn't have the mental capacity to understand what was happening. But somehow, I knew it was very bad. Whatever was happening was very bad. I'll always remember the feeling of being in the car that day. I remember feeling lost and sad. Really, really sad.

When you look back at what had been going on, it was a miracle we were alive at all. After the bathtub incident, Paula had risked her life and my life to tell a teacher what was happening at home. Had Paula not done that, it would've been over. I wouldn't be here telling my story. She was brave. We always had each other's backs as kids. We were inseparable and tight because we had been through so much. We drank toilet water together, we survived together, we tried to fight off Big Mike together. And Gina just couldn't get her shit together. She was the definition of a train wreck.

The night the cops took us away was the night we went to our first foster family. It sucked. We went to the house of a frumpy-looking white lady. She was short, maybe five feet two, and fat with brown curly hair. She wasn't very nice. She fed us, and we watched TV for a bit, and then my sisters and I were separated. The foster lady didn't want us to sleep together. I still don't know why. I went right at her—gave her attitude. She told me to sleep in a different room, but as soon as she went to bed, I went upstairs to hang out with my sisters. My job was to protect them, and that's what I did. And that was the last night we lived together.

8

Foster Care

FOSTER CARE WAS WEIRD. MY SISTERS' FOSTER FAMILIES DIDN'T want me, so we were separated. My social worker was useless. Her name was Melissa. She never did anything—just paraded me around to all sorts of weird families. She told me they were taking me somewhere for a visit. It was really a sneak attack. Social workers did that a lot. They never told me what was coming. Your social worker would say, "Okay, you're gonna go visit with so-and-so," and tell you some shit to get inside your head and make you think it was a good event, and then they'd end up leaving you there. And that was it. You never saw them again. The first time they got me with that crap was with my first foster family. The social worker put me in the car and took me to the Store People. I don't remember their names, but I know they owned a convenience store in Albany, a shitty-looking, hole-in-the-wall store.

The Store People were awful. How these people got approved to foster kids should be one of the seven wonders of the world. They were absolute trash. Their store had tons of candy bars, beverages, newspapers—all the boring shit you'd expect to find at a convenience store. The first thing I did when we visited the store was head to the candy aisle and steal a candy bar. I was hungry. I didn't give a fuck, even at four or five. Going forward, I stole from their store a lot. They never caught me. For some reason they ended up liking me and took me in. But life there was miserable. I ran away three times and got pretty good at it. I think I lasted around twelve hours once. At four or five, I just didn't have what it took to make it longer. I think the cops usually found me down the street and brought me back. I always tried to escape. If you turned your head for a second, I would run. The Store People treated me like shit. They yelled at me. They made me lick my plate. They made me eat off the floor. They told me I was fucked-up, so my birthday didn't count. They said I went back a year or stayed the same age or some bullshit. They took my toys away, and they were constantly putting me down. It was the same shit over and over. And they made me hang out in the convenience store all the time. What a life—five years old, sitting in a convenience store, watching them count cigarettes and read the paper. I just wanted to play. It just wasn't a good fit. Either that, or they eventually had just had enough.

After the Store People, I went to the Pattersons. That was my favorite foster family. They were who I wanted to end up with. They lived in Latham, New York, in a big, nice house on the corner of a block. The mom was an Asian woman, and the dad was a white guy with glasses. They had a few Asian kids, two boys and two girls, in addition to me. They were nice people. I wanted eggs every day, and they would always say I was getting eggs, but then they'd give me Cheerios instead. They gave me a nice room and tons of stuffed animals. For the most part, the kids were nice to me. We got along well. The house was on the same block as some kids I would later to go to high school with, Jeff Griffin and Eddie Higas, though we didn't know we lived on the same block because we were so young. They were the friends I would later go around and smash people's mailboxes with. Sorry, neighbors.

The Patterson lady made this Asian dish from dandelions she found on the side of the road. She would literally stop her car, get out, and pick dandelions for dinner. Then she cooked them with rice. It was fucking amazing. I haven't had it since, but I remember it was the best thing in the world. The Pattersons were extremely nice. They even got me a Power Wheel. I shared it with their other kids. We used to play Ninja Turtles, and we thought the water tower was where the Ninja Turtles really were. I thought I was Rafael. He was rude, so I connected with him the most.

The Pattersons gave me a good life. We children ate well, played with toys, and had friends. There was no yelling or arguing. But they really wanted to move to Miami or South Beach. We flew down to Florida and stayed in a hotel. We went to tour the house they wanted to buy, and it was a shithole. There were lizards all over the thing, inside and outside. It was some hole in the wall that looked like it was in the Glades. But the Pattersons slowly started fixing it up. We spent a lot of time in Miami. Ultimately, they had to make a choice. The state of New York basically said, "You can move to Miami, but you can't have Laz, or you can stay in New York, and you can have Laz." It was a no-brainer. They wouldn't give up Miami for me. Why would they do that? Checkmate. Game over. Finito. No Miami for me. I loved that city, though. I'd love to go back. Maybe I'll have a place there someday. The limited moments I had there were great. It was a beautiful place. Even though I was only five, I remember.

That experience really hurt. The Pattersons had picked a city over a person, and that was always in the back of my mind. I felt like I wasn't important from that point on. As selfish as it sounds, I wanted them to pick me over Miami. But they didn't. They didn't even hesitate. That was the worst part. They were basically like "Yeah, okay, let's sign off on that. Get this kid out of here so we can leave." I mean, what kind of fucking experience is that for a kid? I thought if they really loved me, they'd pick me. But nope. Apparently, being in the sunshine was more important than I was. They could've waited through the adoption process and made it official, and we could've all moved to Miami. It might have taken an extra year. But I wasn't worth it to them. That was a trend in foster care. I always felt like

I didn't belong. Every time I set up shop with a family, I knew it wouldn't last long. I hadn't liked the foster people I'd been sent to stay with until I met the Pattersons. I loved them. But they wanted the pool and palm trees more than they wanted me.

At that time, I was visiting with my mom once a week. I had constant counseling. I had social worker visits. It was annoying being a product of the system. They just bothered me all the time. Half of the social workers were fucking idiots. I thought, *How can they help me? They haven't been through what I've been through. What do they know?* That's what I thought then, not now. Now I understand how important social workers are, and I'd love to get involved in some way. But back then I thought they were fucking stupid. They just got in the way and messed everything up. I had to meet with them all the time. They made me take classes for my anger. And my loser mom wanted to hang out every once in a while. She talked like she was such a big shot. "I'm gonna get you everything. We're gonna be a family. I'm gonna have a car, and you'll have all the toys you want. We're gonna do it. I'm working toward it; it'll just be a little bit longer. Hang in there." That woman lied through her damn teeth.

Meanwhile, I had been living with the Pattersons. They had been great, and I was starting to feel comfortable with them, like we were a real family. But they didn't want me. They wanted Miami instead. So when they pulled the rug out from under me, I had a visit with a new family.

9

Karen and Phil

KAREN AND PHIL CAME TO SEE ME AT THE PATTERSONS' HOUSE. THE Pattersons said, "There are two people who want to meet you." They didn't say anything about me living with them. That's how people in the foster system got you. It was always some sort of kumbaya, "let's make new friends" bullshit instead of the truth. How stupid was I not to figure that out? Karen and Phil visited, and they liked me. They wanted to foster kids. You see where this is going.

First, I had an overnight visit with Karen and Phil. They should've realized then, when I dumped water on their cat, that it wasn't a fit. First I grabbed the cat, and then I grabbed a pitcher and dumped water on the cat. They should've known then and backed away. But you know, they were typical white people who thought they could do all things just because. They thought they could save pathetic, broken kids. They got to tell kids what was best to wear and what to eat and when. They got off on that shit.

Shortly after the overnight visit came the sneak attack. The Pattersons packed up my stuff and put it in their van. I think they told me we were going on vacation or they were taking me to Miami with them or something. Some kind of lie. Instead, they took me to a new foster home—Karen and Phil's.

It was fall. We drove up to the house, and the Pattersons said they were stopping to say hi to a friend. Nope. They took me around to the back of the house by the screened porch, and I looked around at the forest, thinking, *What the hell?* I was used to seeing kids everywhere, to the suburbs. But their house was remote and cut off from the world. And ugly. They had designed it themselves—a weird, triangular-looking thing surrounded by grass and trees, across the street from a river. It wasn't like anything I'd seen before.

I met Phil and Karen again when we got there. They said hi, and I just looked at them. And that was it. The Pattersons peeled me off the leg of one of my foster brothers, and they left. They said, "Bye, Laz! See you later!" Another lie. Game over. No Miami. I never saw them again.

It was weird after the Pattersons left. I didn't say much. I just sat by myself and looked at Karen and Phil. I think I was wearing a blue shirt and gray shorts and some weird shoes—Ninja Turtles or something. They tried to talk to me, but I just didn't know them. They were basically strangers at that point. I was lost.

I woke up the next morning, and they made me eggs. They gave me a big box of toys. Phil gave me a new toy every day. He was great at that. Karen took me to look at the garden. I didn't want to do that. I was a kid. I just wanted to play. But Karen decided we had to look at sunflowers instead. "Isn't is so cool how sunflowers grow in the ground?" Umm … no. I asked if I could go play. She said I could play for a little bit, but then we would have to garden. I said I didn't want to garden. I wanted to play with toys. Karen just bugged me all day. She took me for a walk on the bike path across the street, along the river. In all honesty, I think she tried. We got off on an okay foot. But it just wasn't a good fit. She would've been great for a nerdy farm kid who was into agriculture and wanted to be an Amish person. Or a pilgrim. Karen would've loved that. She even looked like a pilgrim.

Karen was anti-everything—anti-sports, anti-entertainment. She collected newspapers like a hoarder. She kept piles stacked to the ceiling. She'd sit in the living room, and behind her would be stacks and stacks of newspapers. She'd tell Phil she'd be working all day, while he was actually working, but really she'd sleep till ten, have breakfast, watch soap operas at one in the afternoon, and then take a nap until Phil came home. She said she wanted to garden, but then we'd go outside, and she would sit and read a book. She just wanted to tell everyone what to do, but not do it herself.

As soon as I got to their house, they tried to instill their bullshit values of order and discipline. Karen was stuck in the 1960s, and Phil was just a pushover who did what Karen told him. Karen was German—strict as hell. She yelled at everyone for everything. She made me do dumb shit like lay out my clothes the night before. She dressed me like an idiot. Phil got water in the soap dish once, and she flipped the fuck out. She would later make up a stupid story about Phil sitting on my baby sister's head. That shit never fucking happened. She always had an agenda. She made me do all her chores. And they weren't normal chores. I was doing *chores*. We had acres of land, and we were basically running a fucking farm. She hustled me for that and took advantage of me because I could work. I could too. I could always pull my weight, and I did. I farmed acres of land, in between getting yelled at for every little thing.

I was just so fucked in the head at that point. I'd been through so much—three foster families, Gina, Big Mike. I just didn't know how to act. I tried to drown the cat in the toilet. Karen got mad at me and gave me a time-out. I get it. There was nothing wrong with that. One time, I knocked all the bikes down in Sears. They dragged me out of the store. Another time-out. Fine. At first, I just got time-outs, or I stood in the corner for a few minutes. It wasn't bad. Then it switched. They got super strict with everything. Everything I did got me criticized, belittled, and berated. There was always something wrong with me. They told me I had attention deficit disorder, and they told me to suck up my past. "Everybody has problems," they'd say. "No big deal." Really? No big deal? I'm pretty sure Judy didn't try to drown you, Phil. Karen, I know your mom smacked you in the mouth, but you definitely deserved it. My mom smacked me just because I was a dude and she hated men. How was that fair?

The visits with Gina continued. My sisters and I would hang out with Gina what felt like once a month. They'd get us all in a room in some center where fucked-up families would go and pretend to be whole, even though they weren't, because the crackhead mother or father couldn't get their shit straight. So that's what we did. We pretended. Basically, Gina sang kumbaya and said, "We're gonna be a family again. We're gonna be this and that." I was tired of Phil and Karen. They had weird values and made me wear sweaters every day. I was ready to get the fuck out of there and go on to something better. But it wasn't happening.

The social workers took our statements about what had happened—the sexual abuse, Big Mike, all of it. I've never seen those records. I never heard about Big Mike again. Gina was failing. I just wanted to have my mom back and to be able to see my siblings again. Even after all of the abuse and Gina almost killing me, I just wanted us all to be a family. It never happened.

10

Peas

THE FIRST TIME PHIL AND KAREN YELLED AT ME, IT WAS ABOUT their cooking. Karen liked to make homemade mac and cheese. That normally would be fine, but she put peas in it. Who puts peas in mac and cheese? She said, "Look, you're not leaving the table until you eat the peas and the mac and cheese." I didn't want to. I didn't care what she said. I would sit there all night. And I did. It was a standoff, and I held my ground for a long time. They yelled at me and berated me. They just kept going. They made me cry. But I still wouldn't eat it. I didn't want their nasty food. I was thinking, *Get Kraft like normal people, you morons.*

It just got worse from there. One little argument would turn into a showdown, me versus them, every time. And I wouldn't fold. If I missed a chore, they would yell at me and make me write one hundred sentences: "I will do what I'm told and not talk back." I talked back a lot. They'd say, "Why didn't you take out the recycling?" And I'd say, "Well, because you didn't fucking do it." What did they expect? They expected this kid—ripped away from his family, bounced around multiple homes, abused, and beaten—to just get to their house and do what they told him? Why? Why would I listen? Karen tried to run a dictatorship: "You'll do what you're told and not talk back."

At Karen and Phil's, I was yelled at, screamed at, and spanked. Who spanks their kid on the ass? It's so weird. You're literally smacking a minor on the ass. It's perverted. And it doesn't work. Phil would hit me, and I'd hit him back. Karen would hit me, and I'd hit her back too. They hit me for everything. Karen would say, "Do this, or else," and I wouldn't do it. So I would get an ass whupping. It just wasn't working. I didn't belong with this family. And instead of going through the proper channels and reporting it and saying, "Look, this isn't working with Laz—we made a mistake," they just used me to do chores and berated me. They made me shovel compost, feed the cats and dogs, and take care of the chickens, and every day I would get screamed at for forgetting to water one of the animals, because I had only ten minutes before I had to run to get the bus—because if I missed the bus, they'd beat me. I just couldn't do anything right. If I fed the cat, there would be something wrong with the way the food was in the bowl. If I went to get a sandwich, I got yelled at because it was too close to dinner. If someone offered me a cookie, I would get smacked for taking the biggest one. If I had a basketball book, they'd rip into basketball. "Basketball is just a bunch of sweaty men who chase a ball around," they said. They'd tell me their opinion, and if I disagreed, I'd get smacked because it was "rude" for me to have an opinion.

Things just got progressively worse. There were a lot of incidents. One of the memorable ones was when I pegged Phil in the dick with a rock. Karen and Phil and I were going back and forth, and it was starting to get physical. Phil was beating on me. I ran outside. I felt safer out there. Little did I know that I'd just get another beating for going outside. Phil would hit me so hard. After he hit me a few times, I ran around to the front of the house and started pelting the house with rocks. I was mad. I was ready for war. I might lose, but I'd never give up. He was about sixty feet away, and I had a rock in my hand. I threw it and pegged him right in the dick. I hadn't been aiming for it, but I wasn't sad when the rock hit him there either.

It was a once-in-a-lifetime shot. Usually, I'd overthrow, or the rock would go wide, or so on. I missed every target with the house. But somehow, I managed to hit him. He went down, and they called the cops. The cops came out to the house and questioned me and brushed it under the rug.

I ran away from Karen and Phil's once, not for good, though. I came home and was in huge trouble, not only for running but also because I owed a bunch of assignments at school. Karen was mad. I just wasn't good at school. That's what these people didn't realize. Humans aren't all wired the same way. We're not all from perfect homes and perfect lives. School is hard for a lot of people. So what if I was behind a few assignments?

Phil and Karen were the opposite of what I needed. Karen was a hermit who wanted to be left alone. Phil was always working. He had a great work ethic and worked multiple jobs at times just to put food on the table and cater to Karen's needy ass. They were married, but that relationship never should've happened. And honestly, I shouldn't have gone to their house. It was the end for me. Any dreams I had died at that stop. That may sound harsh, and I may lose my parents for this, but I don't care. They knew I would tell this story someday. That's why they made me change my name. They were trying to change the story.

11

Chris

KAREN AND PHIL OFFICIALLY ADOPTED ME IN 1992. I WAS IN THIRD grade. They made me change my name. I didn't want to do it. My name was Lazarus—Laz—and I didn't want to change it. They said I would get picked on for Lazarus. They were right. I was called Lazy Laz mostly, but also Laz the Taz, because I was angry like the Tasmanian Devil. But who cares? Every kid gets picked on. Karen also said that the name Lazarus would hurt my chances of getting into college. WTF? How? Colleges don't care if your name is Sophocles. If you have the grades, and your family has the money, you're in. Karen was a moron. For having two master's degrees, she was a downright moron. I don't care if this upsets her. It should. She shouldn't have made me change my name. I didn't even get to change it to the name I wanted. I wanted to be Joey. Joey was supposed to be my name. Not Chris. Chris just sounds like a noise. I wanted Joey. I wrote Joey on all my stuff. Told all my friends I was Joey. But nope, they chose Chris.

They forced me into a name change. They manipulated me to make things sound acceptable that were not acceptable. Why would I want to change my name to be what they wanted me to be? Why couldn't I be my own person? That's what the adoption was too. I signed a piece of paper that said I had a new mom and dad, and I was just supposed to be okay with it.

Adoption day was fun but also not fun. It was complicated. It was devastating because that was really the end of my chances at being a family with my mom and siblings. I try to always approach life like there's always time left on the clock. I don't quit. But adoption day was a reminder that Gina had quit on me. I didn't want to be with Karen and Phil. I wanted to be with my mom. Knowing that Paula, Kate, Mikey, and I were never going to be a family again was a punch to the stomach. It was officially the end of my relationship with Gina. Even after all she had put me through, I wanted to be a family with her. I hadn't turned on her yet.

At the same time, adoption day was great because I got out of school. I had a ceremony in front of my friends. I got in front of the classroom and told them I was getting adopted. We were kids, so they had no clue what the hell that meant. The teacher made everyone clap and cheer and congratulate me, but I'm sure they had no idea why. Maybe Andy and Joe remember.

The adoption hearing was at 9:00 a.m., so we got up early. The mood in the house was out-of-this-world happy. Karen and Phil actually got along. It was right before my sister Lily was born, but Karen felt good that day. We put on our suits, got in the car, and headed to the courthouse. First, we took pictures outside and around the capital. I hadn't known what a suit was before that day, but now I had a suit on! I felt proud to be wearing it. I felt special for once. People had always taught me I didn't matter, so that's how I acted. I still act that way sometimes. But that day I felt special.

After pictures, we went in and shook hands with Judge Brennan, the judge responsible for my case. He was the best. I immediately liked him. I knew he was an honest person. I don't know how, but I just knew. He made me feel comfortable in the courtroom. He was a true hero—handled my case with class and dignity. He was what every judge should aspire to be. He made me feel so good that day.

The proceeding was light and fun, and he approved my having a family. Of course, he approved the adoption. Karen and Phil were a white family, adopting a white kid, and they had money. On paper, it looked great. She had two master's degrees, and he worked at the airport. The beatings and spankings were just overlooked.

A lot of foster kids just bounce around because they're not wanted, so being adopted was a big deal. It was a chance for me to have something a lot of kids didn't get—a family. And for a little while, I thought it would be a good thing. I thought, *This is my family now. I have a school. I have friends.*

After the ceremony, we shook hands and hugged and took more pictures. Then Karen and Phil took me to a horse stable nearby, where the police horses were kept. Afterward, they took me down the street to a restaurant called Otto's, and I had the biggest steak I've ever had. I think it was chicken-fried steak. It was expensive. It was my first time having a fancy meal like that. They told me, "Get whatever you want—the day is all about you." And at that moment, I was overwhelmed. I didn't feel like I deserved it. I didn't feel worthy, even of a chicken-fried steak. I have never had another one but will always remember that one. It was amazing.

We went home and talked about the day and rejoiced and actually enjoyed each other's company for once. There was no fighting. Karen and Phil got along. There was no animosity, no beatings. It didn't last long, but it sure was nice while it did.

12

Math

WHEN I WAS IN FOURTH GRADE, MS. SPARKS CALLED HOME BECAUSE I owed twenty-one assignments in her math class. I think I had told Karen it was eighteen, but it was really twenty-one. I'd lied to her. She had taken me to TGI Fridays the weekend before Ms. Sparks called because I told her I was getting a good report card. I told her I was getting straight As. She had offered to take me to Fridays and asked if I was getting good grades, and obviously, I said yes. I wanted TGI Fridays. Back then, Fridays was the shit. You got ice cream, a soda, and a nice entrée, and I enjoyed the attention for supposedly getting good grades. I never got praise from Karen. Leave it to Ms. Sparks to blow my cover. She called home to let Karen know I owed twenty-one homework assignments, so Karen drove to school to get me. Well, to be accurate, she made Phil get out of work to drive her because she couldn't drive. What forty-five-year-old doesn't have a driver's license? She was so mad at me. She marched straight back to my classroom. I knew I was in trouble, and I knew it would be an ass whupping. I just didn't know how bad it would be.

When we got in the car, she was mad but talking to me, so I thought maybe I'd be okay. She asked what had happened, and I told her I had done the assignments but forgotten to turn them in. I was a kid. It happens. Whatever. Phil just asked me the same things as

Karen. He did that a lot—just mimicked whatever she did. He didn't have a backbone. So we went around in circles like that a few times. When we got home, Karen yanked me out of the car and threw me onto the garage floor. I'd never been ripped out of a car like that. She threw me on the ground and started pounding me. My head hit the ground so hard. When I bounced up, I couldn't hear at first. My head was ringing. She just kept beating me and yelling, "How could you fucking do this? You owe twenty-one assignments! We went to TGI Fridays to celebrate your report card, and you fucking lied to me?" This wasn't a spanking. She was beating me like a piñata, all because I hadn't done my homework. Because the homework sucked. I don't even remember what it was. That's how irrelevant it was.

13

Praise

I WASN'T USED TO PRAISE GROWING UP. THAT WASN'T A THING. When I grew up, your compliment was "you made it through the fucking day." That was it. You survived. There was nothing positive really. I just tried not to get hit, tried not to get killed. That was the case first at Gina's, where I just had to stay out of Gina's way and hope she was in a good mood, and then in foster care, where people just looked at me like a body. My first family, the Store People, barely even talked to me or looked at me. There was nothing there. The Pattersons were great and complimentary and supportive, but then they moved to Miami. Then I got to Karen and Phil's, and it wasn't a positive environment. Every homework assignment was bad. Karen would sit there and yell at me and basically call me stupid because I didn't understand the homework, especially math. They never told me "good job" or "we're proud of you." That wasn't really a thing. Phil would say things like "great job" at graduation, but it wasn't an everyday thing. No, every day was "you're not good enough" or "you're stupid." I was chastised for every homework assignment. I was chastised every time I dressed funny, looked a certain way, or didn't do a chore the right way. The list goes on. And it didn't matter what I did. If I came home with a C, even if I'd gotten it up from an F, it wasn't good enough. I just didn't like school. I guess I was weird. I didn't see a point to learning algebra. Sue me.

But it wasn't just about school with Karen. Even things like sports were a struggle. Take soccer, for example. I mean, I'd never played soccer. I was just learning the game. And she would stand on the sideline, screaming at me. After the game, we'd get in the car, and she'd yell at me, "Why didn't you fucking hustle? Why didn't you do this or that?" And I'd tell her, "If you think it's so easy, why don't you get out there?" Of course, that would create an issue.

Very rarely would Karen say anything positive, and that was a beating. I took a beating year after year after year after year. The cops eventually told me I'd be dead or in jail for life. Karen told me I'd be a fast-food worker or ditch digger. No offense to those people. It doesn't matter what you do for a living. But Karen made the remarks in a derogatory way, like to tell me I was going to be a failure. I felt like nothing could go my way. Life was like a series of peaks. A normal person would climb up the peak, get an award, climb back down, and keep going. That's not how it worked for me. When I got to the top—had a good day or got a good grade—I'd be slammed back down to the bottom. Karen would say, "You'll never be anything" and tear me down. I used to think I didn't deserve anything. I didn't deserve praise. What would I be praised for? I was worthless. Every day I'd sit there and think, *You're weak, you suck, you're the worst, you can't win. I hate you.* And I'd just go after myself in my own head. I was hurt. I got my ass kicked every day—mentally, physically, emotionally—and it got to a point where I just didn't care about life. I was like "Fuck it, I don't care anymore. Just take me." It was sad. But it also made me angry.

I thought everything I did would be a failure. And it would be all my fault. I had been beaten down so many times that I was almost conditioned not to expect to do well. Anytime I would think something positive, I would talk myself out of it. Karen's voice would be inside my head, telling me, *Nope. You're not worthy. Just give up.* There were so many times I wanted to talk to a girl, but I'd get inside my head and think, *There's no fucking way you're even close to good enough for her. You're not even a person. You're just a piece of shit. She'd never like you. You're an idiot. You got a 19 on an exam one time. Don't even fucking try.* I thought the same thing with jobs. I'd want to apply for a job, but I'd think, *No, you're not good enough. You'll never get that job, you piece of shit.* That mentality came from Gina, who had beaten my ass every day and whipped me with her belt and made me eat my own vomit. And it came from Karen, who hit me and berated me and made me feel like I wasn't worthy of love. I didn't think I was worthy of anything. People would thank me or compliment me or say something simple, like "have a good day," and I would get so mad. I'd think, *What the fuck does it matter if I have a good day?* because I just didn't know how to accept positivity. People would wish me a happy birthday, and I would be skeptical of their motives. I'd think, *Do they really want me to have a happy birthday, or are they just saying that and really hoping I fail?* I always had low expectations for my birthday, thanks to Karen.

She used to ground me on my birthday—not just once, but multiple years. One time she grounded me for eight months for one offense, after I got suspended at school. Some kid tried to steal out of my bookbag, so I rocked him. I hit him, and I just kept hitting him. I was already angry because of the shit that I had to deal with at home, so when Trent tried to reach in my bag, I snapped. I know he remembers, because I knocked him into next month. I went to the principal's office, and they called my parents. My dad picked me up from school, and he was cool in the car. He asked me what had happened, and I told him, "That kid tried to steal from me." I don't even remember what was in my backpack. I think it was a Walkman. Or a Discman. One of those ancient relics that used to be the shit. If you had one of those in school, you were balling. My dad was pretty understanding about the situation. He said something like "Shit happens. I gotta go back to work, so you'll have to deal with your mom." And I thought, *Great, I'm done. I'm gonna get hit.* By some sort of miracle, she didn't hit me when I got home. She just wanted to humiliate me and kill my dignity, so she made me call the kid and apologize, even though he'd started the fight. She didn't want to hear my side of the story at all. I know I was wrong for hitting the kid, but she didn't even bother to listen to see if I had been wrong. Then she told me I was grounded. First, it was six months, and then she extended it to eight. EIGHT. For most kids, being grounded meant not being able to watch TV or hang out with friends for a few weeks. Not with Karen. When Karen grounded me, it was like living in federal prison. She took everything out of my room, even my posters. Have you seen *Shawshank*? Even Andy Dufresne had a poster. But Karen took everything I had. Anything basketball-related was gone. Any books were gone. Any hope was gone.

14

Twin Lakes

IT WAS THE SUMMER OF 1998. MOST KIDS WERE ENJOYING SUMMER, taking vacations with their families or hanging out with their friends. Not me. I was in summer school. No fun was allowed at my house. Instead, my lovely "parents" sent me to a mental hospital.

I was sent there for threatening to kill myself. I'd had enough. There had been another fight with Karen and Phil. I was outside throwing rocks at the house and at Phil. I feel bad about that now. I'm not sure what he was doing, but he didn't deserve that. Of course, he and Karen called the cops. I threatened to kill myself, so they called an ambulance too. First, the paramedics took me to a mental treatment facility to determine if I was really suicidal. When I got there, the staff did all my paperwork. It took hours. Then they asked me all sorts of questions. I lied in my answers. Of course, I wanted to kill myself. But I didn't tell them that. I knew it wouldn't end well if I told them the truth. They asked if I wanted to kill myself, and I said no. They asked a few more times, and I said no each time. So they figured, *Okay, he's not a threat to kill himself, but he's definitely fucked-up, so we'll send him to Twin Lakes mental hospital upstate.*

Twin Lakes was great—chicks everywhere, basketball, and group sessions all day. There was anger management, meditation, and all sorts of other useless group chats to pass the time. The food was buffet-style. If you know me, you know I love a buffet, and that is probably because of my time at Twin Lakes. I had a cool roommate. He was a big dude. He made me a Nas poster with "Hate Me Now" on it, which was my favorite song.

Everything at Twin Lakes was structured. The staff members were strict but nice. I met some interesting people and a lot of strange people. I guess they probably thought the same about me. One chick told me I was ugly and my eyes looked retarded. Nice girl. To be honest, the group sessions didn't help me at all. I was depressed beyond belief, and sitting in a circle sharing my feelings wasn't going to change that. I answered the questions right so I could leave on my own terms. But nothing was accomplished.

Twin Lakes was something like a couple hundred dollars or a thousand dollars a day. Karen and Phil reminded me of that all the time. They would say things like "You need to hurry up with your treatment because this is expensive." Nice, right? They should've just said, "Why don't you speed up your rehab process? I know you're fucked in the head, but it's pricey, and we don't actually care about your mental health, so pick up the fucking pace." I wanted to stay at Twin Lakes forever. The food was all-you-can-eat. I got to play basketball. I had friends. It was great. But man, that place was weird too. There was a girl named Billie Jo who would walk up to the window and just stare at you for minutes at a time. She looked like she wanted to kill you. The other kids were always having mental breakdowns. People would fight. I was there because I wanted to kill myself, but a lot of other people were there for drugs. Still, I would've rather stayed there than live with Karen and Phil.

15

Baseball Bat

THE FIRST BIG ARGUMENT I HAD WITH KAREN AND PHIL WAS IN 1998. Great year—the Bulls won. They won every year back then. Things at home were getting bad at that point. We got physical on an almost daily basis. I was getting hit constantly. Phil spanked me, and Karen slapped me with an open palm, usually on the face, but sometimes on my back too. It was always about homework. The teachers would load us up with homework because they were bullies. Ours were, anyway. And Karen was a drill instructor with homework. "It better be perfect. It better be neat. Show your work." And I just didn't understand it. I didn't get math. I've always been a visual learner. I need someone to show me how to do something in order to learn it and retain it. Otherwise, I just see words on a page, and I don't get it. Don't even get me started on IKEA directions. Those look like hieroglyphics. I just take one look at them and give up.

I used to come home and spend hours studying and doing homework, but I'd still fail my tests—or my classes altogether. I had a pretty low grade in math. I kind of lost hope with school. I was starting to lose hope overall, really. We fought at home every day. It was so distracting. I couldn't concentrate on school. I'd be at school just thinking about going home and getting physical and getting hit—and hitting back and threatening. At that point I threatened to hurt Karen during our fights. So you can imagine how toxic that environment was. And I was going to school every day with kids who weren't dealing with that. They had no idea what it was like to be physically or mentally tortured by their parents. Lucky kids. So I'd go to school and just sulk. All these kids were living such good, boring, normal lives. I wanted to be like them. So many cool kids, man. I was so excited to be at Woodrow Roosevelt High School. But I was sad inside. Every day at home, I was getting beaten on and yelled at and destroyed—over homework! Who cares about algebra? I've been out of school for a long time, and I've never used algebra at a job. And somehow, I'm still doing pretty well.

One night, I wasn't getting a math problem. Something that should've been easy for a parent to help their kid with turned into a fight. It was a tough night. I was literally just putting numbers on the page to say I'd shown my work, so I could get enough points to maybe eke out a sixty-five. And Karen just kept berating me. "What don't you get? How do you not understand this? Are you ever gonna get this?" A lot of times she would hit me on the head. So I was anticipating it. I was ready, bracing myself for the blow. "Do you even care?" she asked me. I responded, "No, I don't. I just want to go to bed." She yelled back, "Get up there now and do your fucking homework!"

I grabbed my book, and as I walked by her, she smacked me in the back of the head. And that was it. That was the moment everything changed, and I had just had enough. That's when I turned into angry me. She smacked me on the back of the head, and I turned around and gave her a look. It was supposed to be a warning look so she would leave me alone. I was trying to stop it from getting physical that day. I never wanted it to get physical. But she just kept yelling at me and insulting me. She always said such mean shit to me. I glared at her, walked past her, went upstairs, slammed my bedroom door shut, and punched the bunk bed. I was fuming. I went to the back left corner of the room, by the dresser. The dresser was between two windows—one facing the road and one facing the side of the house. And I just stood there in the corner, between the dresser and the window, trying to calm down. I was thinking, *Fuck, man, this is the worst. I'm failing math, and I don't get it. I don't know how much more I can take. I don't want to be here. I just want to die. Why didn't Gina kill me? Why didn't she just hold my head under the water a little bit longer? This could all be over, and I wouldn't ever have to get hit over math or because I had a typo again.* I just didn't want to be on this earth anymore. It was homework. It shouldn't have turned into a battle because I didn't get it. It was just numbers on a page. Ms. Sparks, my fourth-grade teacher, had known that. She had taught me division step-by-step. She had taken the time to understand my learning style. Karen never did that. She didn't care about my learning style. She expected me to get it and be smart and ace all my classes. I was just so depressed that I didn't care about homework. I was thinking about running away or killing myself. I don't think I was suicidal, but I always thought about how I didn't want to be alive anymore. I just felt lost. I had no friends, my mom was gone, and no one liked me. I felt invisible. I felt like I didn't exist.

Karen stormed up the stairs, yelling at me the entire time, and barreled through the door into my room. She started taunting me. At this point I was blacked-out mad. I was red—or green, like the Hulk. It was DEFCON 1. She was in my room, my space. The minute she'd come through the threshold into my space, she was a threat. That's how I thought, because of Big Mike. I would try to get ready for him to attack so I could fight back. Anyone coming into my room was seen as the enemy. When Karen stormed into my room, my first thought was *There's an intruder in my space, and I'm in danger.* I was anticipating that she would swing at me and was planning my counterpunch to her face. I would beat her head like a piñata.

She kept taunting me. She got in my face and said, "What are you gonna do? Huh?" She was shaking her fists at me in an uppercut motion, like she wanted to fight. She cornered me. I was up against the corner, between the dresser and the windows, trying my best to keep it from getting physical. But she just kept coming toward me, shaking her fists like she wanted to punch me. And when she got close enough, I snapped. I grabbed her by the collar and threw her against the dresser. She screamed, slammed into the wall, and fell to the floor. I'll never forget the scared look on her face as she fell. I could tell she hadn't been anticipating that type of power. Usually, she would hit me, and I'd do my best not to hit back. I hit back occasionally, but most of the time I didn't hit back. What was the point? I didn't want to turn everything into a hitting match. But that day, she was asking for it. She had come into my room when I was trying to calm down and had gotten in my face and taunted me. And I'd had enough. She shrieked, her glasses fell onto the floor, and I warned her, "If you fucking put your hands on me again, I'll fucking kill you." I slammed her against the wall and yelled, "Don't fucking touch me again!" She looked so pathetic up against the wall.

Phil came running in when he heard Karen shrieking. I broke from Karen, and Phil and I started wrestling. He was killing me. He was crushing me. He had me in some kind of move—I don't know what it was. I just knew as soon as he let up, I was going to get him. He was getting the better of me, but I kept going.

The fight between Phil and me spilled into the hallway. Out of the corner of my eye, I saw Karen coming toward my weak side with a baseball bat in her hand. She raised it up and got ready to swing at me. I had to protect myself from the baseball bat, so I elbowed her in the mouth, and she started bleeding. She ended up with two black eyes and a broken nose. That's what she got for trying to attack me with a baseball bat. Phil and I were still fighting, and he was still winning. We rolled into his room, then stood up and yelled at each other. Eventually, I got him back. I broke his nose and punched his eye. I pounded him. Then he got on top of me on the bed and pinned me down. I dug my nails into his face. I was willing to die for this fight. I didn't care. Why would I care about my life? No one else cared about it. I dug my nails in deeper and tried to peel his face back, and he got off. He said something like "Damn, you should be in wrestling" or boxing or something.

Phil and Karen threatened to call the cops but didn't. I went to my room and went to bed. After something like that, you know it's never going to be the same again—it's just not. The relationship was gone. It never got to a point where it was good or decent. It was just animosity and hatred. I hated all of them. I hated Karen, and I hated Phil. Okay, maybe I just really disliked Phil. I put up with him. He's a good dude. There's just a lot of me that resents him for having me arrested.

16

The Arrest

PHIL AND I ARGUED AGAIN THE NEXT MORNING. I DON'T REMEMBER why. But I went at him again. I said, "Fuck you. I'm not listening to you. You're not my dad. Get the fuck outta here." Same shit, different day. I left the house and got on the bus. I thought it would be a normal day. I'd go to school, come home, and do it again the next day. I knew I was grounded for the rest of my life after our fight, but whatever. They had taken basketball from me. They knew it meant everything to me, and they'd taken it. I had nothing to look forward to. I used to go home after school and think of ways to kill myself. That was my hobby. That's why mental health is so important. We need to pay attention to what's going on with the youth.

I went to school, and around 9:00 a.m. I was called to the principal's office. I think she was in her fifties. She had blonde hair and was kind of short. I remember she was wearing yellow that day. Nice lady. I asked her why I was there, and she said, "Did you have a disagreement with your parents?" I said, "Yeah, last night." She got up from her desk and told me to wait in her office for a minute.

After she left the room, two cops came in to get me. That was a fucking shock. The cops said I was being arrested for third-degree assault. They read me my rights, told me to turn around, and put handcuffs on me, right there in the principal's office. Then they led

me out of school in front of the entire student body. It was humiliating. My friends probably saw it. It ruined any reputation I had at
Woodrow Roosevelt High. The cops tightened my handcuffs to the
point that I could barely feel my hands. Then they threw me in the
back of the police car and took me to the station.

The cops were assholes. They taunted me in the car the whole
way to the station. "Who the fuck do you think you are, not listening
to your parents? Disrespecting them? Are you some kind of fucking
punk? Think you're a tough guy, huh?" They totally didn't know
what had happened. Fucking power-tripping lowlifes. I know there
are some good cops out there, but these weren't the good kind.

When we got to the police station, they handcuffed me to the
desk and started my paperwork. They taunted me some more with
the same shit they had been saying in the car on the way over. Phil
came to the station while I was handcuffed to the desk, and then
he started talking shit too. He felt safe because he knew I couldn't
do anything. I was literally chained to the desk. I'll never forget
that moment. He had to handcuff me to talk shit, because he knew
if I hadn't been handcuffed, I would've killed him. Fucking pussy.
Fucking nerd thought he could talk shit to me.

The cops finished their paperwork and put me back in the car to
take me to court. Once again, they made my handcuffs way too tight
and taunted me in the car the whole way. "Who do you think you are?
You think you got all the answers? Someday you're gonna be in the
big house, and you're gonna regret not listening to your parents." But
they didn't know my story. Ignorant idiots. When we arrived at the
courthouse, they put me in a holding cell with shackles and handcuffs.
Shackles! I was just a kid. Then they paraded me out of my cell, shackles
and handcuffs still on, and into the courtroom for my sentencing. I pled
guilty to third degree assault. The judge ordered thirty days at a detention center. I thought, *What the fuck is a detention center?* Normally,
you'd just put your head on the desk for an hour after school, and you'd
be done. I didn't know what the hell a detention center was.

17

Hudson Detention Center

THE HUDSON DETENTION CENTER WAS ACTUALLY A HOUSE ON THE outskirts of Albany, in the middle of nowhere. It was so nerve-wracking. I knew when I got there that I wasn't going home anymore. This was it. I was scared. I was one of the only white kids there at the time. When I walked in, everyone looked me over, sizing me up. This type of world was all competition. A lot went on behind the scenes that staff members didn't know about—fights left and right, drugs, anything. We snuck it all in. I got punched in the face for looking at a kid named Jim Greene. He was a Crip. He didn't like the way I looked at him, so he punched me in the face. I was locked up with people who claimed they were Crips, Bloods, Latin Kings, all the gangs. And I was the only white kid. I didn't fit in. It was a game of survival. Thankfully, all the black kids took me under their wing, not at first, but eventually. I smashed a kid in the head with a rock because he said something mean, and he was about to hit me with a massive jar, but the staff members stopped him before he could get me. That was my initiation. That was my "in" with the other guys in the house.

The guys and I played basketball, ate, and had school. We were in the house basically 24-7, except from three to five every afternoon. That was outside time. We played basketball, football, and so on. I was the only kid who had to shave. You had to get special permission to shave. And they monitored you while you did it. You had no privacy. The showers were either cold water or hot water. There was no warm. You had to decide if you wanted to burn or freeze. You showered once a week. Soda was a privilege that you earned for good behavior. All meals were scheduled. You ate three times a day. You had no time for yourself. None.

I was almost done with my thirty-day sentence, and right before my court date, one of the idiot kids in the house tested me. I think he stole something of mine. I punched him in the face, maybe six times, in the bathroom. The staff members were so confused about why I would jeopardize my court case. I was worried I'd fucked it up. Thankfully, it didn't affect my case. I got out of the group home, went back to Karen and Phil's, and went back to Woodrow Roosevelt High. I was treated like garbage at Woodrow Roosevelt. It just wasn't the same. They treated me like I was OJ Simpson. My reputation was ruined. I had pretty much known that would happen when those asshole cops handcuffed me and dragged me out in front of the whole school. I was lost. I don't know what people said. I don't know if people even knew who I was before that point. If they did know me, they got a different look at me. I remember that one kid with red hair, Rick Kelley, said some mean shit to me. He'd heard I hit my parents and got in my face about it—made fun of me. It was cold. No one liked me. No one cared. My home life was horrible. It was good for the first month or two after Hudson, but then it went back to the same shit. It was just yelling at first. Then the physical violence started up again. I just kept getting hit. I'd hit back occasionally. On and on it went.

The following summer, I spiraled.

18

Dictionary

Eventually, it got to a point where Karen and I couldn't be in the same room together. She just hit me every day. And she did this thing where she would talk shit to me but hide behind Phil, like he could protect her. Psh. I was locked up the final time around November, right around election time. We had gotten increasingly violent. We hit each other and threatened each other. I threatened to kill Karen. It was dark.

I was doing homework one day—a school paper, I think—and I didn't know what a word meant. I asked Karen and Phil, and they mocked me. They told me, "Look it up in the dictionary, idiot! You should get this. Look it up. Don't be an idiot." All sorts of mean shit like that. I looked up the word in the dictionary and read the definition out loud, but I think I mispronounced it. And somehow that turned into an argument. I can't remember if I was at fault here. I might have been. I might've started it off.

Phil mocked me for saying the word wrong. He asked something like, "Did you seriously just mispronounce it? Are you kidding?" and implied that I was a fucking idiot. He shoved the dictionary in my face, so I slammed the dictionary out of his hand. I smacked the book down and shoved him back, away from me. I got mad and said, "I'm ready. We can do this right now." I was trying to get him to fight me. Karen was behind him, talking shit, and I looked at her and said, "Bitch, I will fucking kill you." And I meant it.

She got really scared. I was going to do it too. I wanted to shut her up so much. After all the shit she'd put me through, I'd had enough. She was lucky that Phil was blocking her that day. I hit Phil, threatened Karen, and went outside and started destroying their property. I threw rocks at the house. I tore down part of the big wooden fence that went around the yard. I dared Karen to come out so I could fight her. She wouldn't. She was too scared to face me. She just sat there and watched while I lost my shit.

From then on, any niceties were gone. It was over. We would argue all day, every day. They couldn't beat me. I wouldn't stop. I would not give up. In my mind, I was protecting myself from potential threats—Phil and Karen. I threatened Karen night and day. I snapped at her anytime she spoke to me. I didn't want anything to do with her. She would say something to me, and I'd turn to her and say, "Don't fucking talk to me." I'd disappear for hours at a time to go play basketball. The basketball court was the only place I felt safe and like I could be myself. In school, I was getting scores of 6 on exams. I was physically there, but I wasn't mentally there. I think a few of my friends knew I was in trouble. I had nothing left. I was just tired, tired of getting hit and yelled at and beaten on constantly.

I'd had enough. Phil and Karen hit me all the time, and I just wanted to hit back. I wanted to hit them even if they didn't hit me first. That's how angry I was. I just wanted to hurt them. Karen played the most fucked-up mental games with me. I'm telling you, she would absolutely mind-fuck me every day—and Phil too. She came after him for the dumbest shit. He got water in the soap dish once, and she yelled at him. That's the type of shit she decided to make a big deal about. I'd get yelled at if I didn't pick up my room fast enough or if I drank the last of the orange juice in the fridge or some other bullshit. She just yelled at me and hit me all the time. They both did. And after everything I'd been through, I'd just had enough. And at that point, they had fucked up. They couldn't contain me anymore. They couldn't beat me. I was too big. And I was fed up. I went at them all the time. I let them have it every chance I got.

After the dictionary incident, I couldn't go home by myself. Karen was scared of me and didn't want to be alone with me, so she made a rule that I couldn't come home after school. Phil had to pick me up from school and take me to his office, every day. And I would just sit there and wait until it was time for him to go home. I wouldn't get home until six thirty, and when I got home, I was a prisoner in my own house. That's no kind of life for a kid.

19

The Camper

I CAME HOME FROM SCHOOL ONE DAY, AND—YOU GUESSED IT—
Karen and I started yelling at each other. I don't even know what we
were yelling about. We always yelled at each other. We hated each
other. We yelled over everything. It didn't matter what she said to
me; I always said something back. And at that point it was aggres-
sive. I had already broken Phil and Karen mentally. They couldn't
do anything to me that they hadn't already done. I had taken all
their ass whuppings, and the tide was turning. I was becoming a
strong young male, and I was ready to fuck people up. And they
knew it. They knew their time was coming to an end. I was threatening Karen and telling her I was going to kill her or hurt her. I'd
say things like "You have to go to sleep sometime. And that door
doesn't lock." Really awful shit. Karen and I couldn't even be in the
same room at that point—I was forbidden to be alone in the same
room with her.

One night, we were yelling, and I started threatening Karen. It
was getting heated, so I left and walked to the basketball court. I
needed some time to cool off and decompress. I was trying to calm
down, so the situation didn't get physical or go too far. So I went to
the basketball court, which was about a mile away. I did that a lot.
Anytime I had to get out of the house, I'd go to the basketball court

and clear my head. That night, I went back home around 8:30 or 9:00 p.m. When I got home, the doors were locked. They'd locked me out, and I had nowhere to go. I was lost. I went into the camper in the driveway, and they had put sheets in the camper for me. How nice of them, right? I was locked out of my own home. They had left me a blanket, and I slept practically outside in the freezing cold. It was like thirty-two degrees, and I don't even think I had a hoodie. Maybe I did. I don't know. But I know it was freezing, and I wasn't allowed in my own house. Karen didn't think it was a big deal at the time. She didn't see it as child abuse, which it was. She thought that it was an acceptable punishment and I should just get over it. Psh. Maybe she should've been shoved in a fucking camper in thirty-something-degree temperatures. Maybe then she would see how fucked-up it was.

Karen made me sleep in the camper for a few nights after that. I was no longer allowed to sleep in the house. I think somebody at school found out that I was sleeping in a camper. I can't remember if I told Dev and he told somebody. But I know I told somebody, and that person told a teacher. Karen got a call home about it. She denied everything, but she did it. It was a problem. It was a fucking problem. I was arrested again shortly after that.

20

The Second Arrest

KAREN AND PHIL MADE THE ULTIMATE SNEAK-ATTACK BITCH MOVE. They didn't tell me it was coming. They went to court and arranged to have me picked up by the police and taken away for good, not to return home. Can you believe that? My own parents snitched on me. We couldn't talk it out first? They couldn't give me a heads-up that this was it? They were cowards, both of them. They quit on me. They went to the cops on their own son and said, "Here, take him."

I was sitting outside when the cop came to the house to arrest me. I could've run. I'd run before. I was fast too. I'd gotten pretty far once. I thought about doing it again, but I knew this was the end. I knew I had fucked up one too many times. That's all it was. Anytime I messed up, I knew. I thought, *Here I go, fucking up again.* I'd always think that. Because of what I'd been through—with Gina, Big Mike, the Store People, the Pattersons, Karen and Phil—I just assumed that anything that went wrong was my fault. When my face hit the bottom of the bathtub at four years old, it had shocked me for life. To this day, I can't understand why people like me. I don't feel it. It took me years to feel my wife's love for me. Incidents like that just take so much out of you. And people don't realize that. They think, *Oh, everybody's got shit to deal with—get over it.* How can you really tell someone that? You don't know what other people have been through. There are some types of pain you just can't "get over." You just have to pretend you're fine so you don't make people uncomfortable. It's bullshit.

The police officer got out of his squad car, looked at me, and said, "You know why I'm here?" I said, "Yeah, I do." I knew it was over. It was the only time I didn't fight. I just took it lying down. He asked, "Do I have to cuff you?" and I said no. He could tell I wasn't going to fight it. He didn't handcuff me, and he let me sit in the front seat of the squad car. It was a pretty quiet ride. He asked me a few basic questions. At one point he said, "You don't seem like they described you." I said, "I'm not." He knew I wasn't a bad kid. He was a nice guy, much nicer than the cops who had arrested me the first time. He dropped me off at the station, shook my hand, and told me, "Good luck."

From there I went to juvie for a couple of days. It was basically county jail, but for kids. The buildings were right next to each other. They treated me like an animal there. That's where I got the chip on my shoulder. From then on, I had my edge. They treated me like a dog. They stripped me naked, they searched me, and they talked shit to me. Back then I was 150 pounds, tops, and surrounded by big 300-pound dudes. I wouldn't be able to do shit against them. I knew I couldn't fight back or try to protect myself, because I would lose. I was literally a caged animal, all thanks to the bullshit that Karen and Phil had started. That's where I ended up, in a cage, essentially. I got lucky. I didn't have to stay in juvie for long. I went back to court, where I had the same judge from the first go-round. He sent me back to Hudson for the time being, until they could figure out a more permanent "home" for me.

21

Birthday

I HAD JUST GOTTEN TO HUDSON. I KNEW I WASN'T GOING BACK
home from there. This was my last strike. I had done enough and
fought back too many times. And the judges, courts, group homes,
and so on always took the parents' side instead of listening to what
the kid had to say. So of course, Hudson took Karen and Phil's side
and looked at me like "get outta here, you animal!" Hudson was
never meant to be a long-term solution, so after two months there,
I had to find somewhere else to go.

While at Hudson, I tried to get scouted by other institutions. I
was trying to get noticed by Bristol Ranch. That was another place
for kids who weren't wanted. There was also a really nice group home
that everyone wanted to go to. I can't remember the name. But it was
bougie. It was co-ed. It was in the Adirondacks somewhere. That's
what I'd heard. I don't know how true that was. Might have been
fantasy land. I'd never find out.

I kept hoping to get noticed, but nothing was happening. I
didn't know where I was going next, but I was ready to get there.
Hudson was good if you were there for a month or so, but anything
longer than that was awful. There was lots of immaturity, a lot of
kids with drug issues, and lots of violence and fighting. They put
all these kids with unstable backgrounds together in one home, and

they didn't get along. They even had kids from rival gangs in the house. And they expected everyone to have some kind of order or structure. Wasn't gonna happen.

My savior was a guy named Aaron Marks. For some reason I thought his name was Scott Marks, but it was actually Aaron. This guy was an angel. He came to Hudson to check out Darryl Brunson, one of my best friends. Darryl was a really good kid who had just gotten mixed up with the wrong crowd at his high school. When Aaron came to Hudson to chat with Darryl, he noticed me. Why would he notice me? Who the fuck knows? That's one of the wonders of the world I just can't figure out. Why would he care about me? I was no one at the time. I had nowhere to go. I couldn't go home. They had given me a break and hadn't sent me to county, but I didn't know where to go now. Aaron noticed me and talked to me. He asked me some questions. I can't remember how I answered them. I knew he was there for another kid, so I figured, *Meh, I'll give it a shot and try to look as composed as possible*, even though my anger was off the charts then. If you looked at me the wrong way, I wanted to fight. Aaron reached out to Hudson and the courts a few days later and said he was interested in taking me on—over Darryl. He picked me over Darryl! He had come there for Darryl. Darryl was a way better kid than me. He was an athlete, a great football player. He was a truck, man—six feet and 250 pounds yet ran like a deer. Fast kid. I miss him. Darryl would end up going to the same place as me, just a few months after Aaron took me.

After Aaron picked me, things started moving rapidly. Not rapidly enough, though. It was the end of the year. You always panicked at the end of the year, because you knew the courts were going to close for the holidays. You had to figure this shit out before the courts closed, because spending the holidays at Hudson was the worst. It was literally hell. You were there with maybe one or two other kids, and you got nothing. You ate grilled cheese on Christmas and just sat there, wasting away. So wherever you were going, you wanted to get there as quickly as possible.

That didn't happen for me. The process took forever. I spent my birthday in November and Christmas the following month at Hudson, locked up for something I hadn't done. Okay, maybe I did something, and maybe I was wrong, but Karen had instigated it, and I had just defended myself. They had created an unstable home environment, and I had defended myself from their beatings, yet I was the one rotting away in the group home, alone. Imagine sitting by yourself on your birthday and Christmas, your favorite holiday, with people who don't give a fuck about you. That's what it was like.

I knew my birthday was going to be bad. Anytime you had to celebrate anything in the group home, it was bad. You didn't get a lot. You didn't get letters or cards. You definitely didn't get presents. I'd been down this road before. Karen and Phil drove out that day to visit me. I honestly thought I might get something from them—a birthday gift or something. And I was actually kind of excited for the visit. Kind of. We started talking, and it was fine at first, but then Karen started up with her usual tough talk. She tried to size me up, tell me I was worthless, say I deserved to be alone on my birthday. I wanted to hit her right there. She said, "Back in my day, you wouldn't be able to walk again right now, because my mom would've put you through a wall." And I said something along the lines of "Look, back in your day, I would've put her through a wall, then put everybody else through the wall too and killed them." Or something like that. Karen flipped her lid. She said, "You are an absolute menace. This place isn't strict enough. You need to go somewhere stricter." Then she plopped a magazine down on the table and said, "Here, happy birthday." That was my birthday gift. It was a *Slam* basketball magazine. And she had put a sticky note on it that said, "Happy Birthday." I thought, *Wow, you just don't care at all.* I was in a group home. That was the one time I was gonna be greedy. I had nothing. I wanted a birthday gift, or at the very least, I wanted my "parents" to pretend to care about me for one day. I was locked up, and they'd had a chance to bring me a present, and they'd brought me a fucking magazine.

I had nothing in the group home. We all ate government cheese. The group home was a nonprofit, so they got all their food from food banks. We ate well for the most part. They got tons of food. Twelve growing kids, plus staff, made for a huge grocery order. We ate chicken, mac and cheese, tater tots, and burgers. But the cheese was disgusting. Government cheese sucks.

We were all behind in school. I actually thought I was going to fail a grade and never graduate high school. I thought I was fucked. I thought I was becoming a loser like Gina. I assumed it was just in my DNA to be a failure. And Karen showed up with a magazine. What a piece of shit. Can you imagine doing that to your kid? They're going through a tough time, and they're doing the best they can, and you throw a magazine at them and call it a day. Unbelievable. I'll never forget that birthday.

Maybe things have changed, but back then group homes weren't rehab facilities. They didn't care about your growth. They just cared that you didn't kill anyone. And it was survival of the fittest. The staff didn't catch a lot of shit. I was getting pegged, hit, and fucked up. I was putting up with all that and waiting for my court case. And Karen brought me a fucking magazine. I never went home again. That was the worst birthday I've ever had. It was the loneliest. I just remember thinking, *Why am I here?* I hated my life. I just wanted to end it so badly.

But Aaron saved me from all of that. He gave me exactly what I needed. He took such good care of me.

22

Valley View

AARON PICKED ME UP FROM HUDSON ON JANUARY 3, 2000, AND took me to Valley View, another group home. That group home was my final place in terms of being locked up—or being "in the custody of the state," or whatever gentle term they want you to use. But if you're not free, you're locked up. So that's what I call it. Valley View was a group home in one of the most racist counties in New York. So much racism. Population: not much. Sleepy Hollow school district. It was in the middle of nowhere and known for its dirt roads and closures.

Compared to Hudson, Valley View Group Home was a totally different world. It was less structured than Hudson, but the kids were more annoying. I was lost when I got there. I got in a fight in the first few days. Some kid wanted to test me and steal my Burger King, and there was no way I was going to let that happen. So I had to jaw him real quick. I punched him right in the face.

Karen didn't visit me at Valley View a lot. Even then we had issues. She refused to visit. Phil would come by himself sometimes and take me to UNO Pizzeria. He was decent. He's a decent human being. He would go out of his way to make sure that I could get a nice meal and feel like a person. Karen just didn't give a fuck.

She rarely visited—said she felt threatened. She was the one who'd
beaten on me! How did she feel threatened? It was insane.

The group home will forever be in my heart. I had some tough
days, but it wasn't their fault. I was just trying to navigate the world
with eleven guys with totally different personalities. They were all
there for fucked-up reasons. Basically everybody had an anger problem. I spent a lot of time trying to learn about the staff members. I
was in a racist town that hated minorities but lived in a house with
almost all minorities. I had to have their backs. I had to prove myself
to the gangs so I could fit in as one of the top people in the house.

Valley View was a decent-sized house with two floors and five
bedrooms. The kitchen was the first thing you saw when you walked
into the house. The laundry room was off to the left, and there was
an office down the hall, right by the stairs. The living room and
den were past the office. The dining room was on the other side of
the kitchen. It had a table big enough for twelve. The second floor
was just bedrooms. Everyone at the group home had a bunkmate or
roommate. The rooms were all different sizes. One fit three beds, but
most fit two. We had pretty comfortable conditions. Residents got
a dresser, a closet, and tons of storage. Most of my roommates were
pretty cool. A couple were weird. You had to keep one eye open at
all times. At any time, you could get jumped. Someone would try to
attack from behind or steal your food or some other bullshit. That
was something that was just bound to happen. You were gonna get
fucked up in the group home. The group home definitely taught me
toughness and how to overcome. We had plenty of fighters.

On a typical day, we'd get up early. Five thirty was the first
wake-up call. There were three or four showers in the house but
twelve kids, and we had only an hour until we had to be outside to
catch the bus. We had to be downstairs by six thirty, so you had to
either have a quick first step or get up early. I would get up at five to
get in the shower before anyone else. We each had a chore to do in
the morning—nonnegotiable. Then came breakfast. We all had to

get our own breakfast. Picture twelve kids at the same time getting ready and getting breakfast. We all had different routines, but we made it work. It was a beautiful thing. Man, some of those guys were like my brothers. I would pick them over anybody in corporate America. At least they would let me know where we stood and not play games with me.

We had to be on the bus by 6:41 a.m. If you missed the bus, you were in trouble. We'd get on the bus and go to school together every morning—Sleepy Hollow High School. It was us against the world out there. We were not liked. Everywhere we went, we were stared at. People talked shit about us. People hated us. We were what the community wasn't. We were the bad boys. We were fucked-up. We were the end of their peaceful existence. They labeled us thugs. They called all my friends the N-word, all of them. It was tough. I liked the group home, but dealing with Sleepy Hollow was the worst experience. I was a white kid, but all my friends were black. I was stuck between wanting to help my friends and needing to look out for myself. I thought, *Yeah, you just called my friend the N-word. We go to a racist school. But I can't do anything, because if I touch anybody, they'll ship me off to something worse, back to county or Bristol.* And Bristol was basically county. There wasn't room for mistakes at Sleepy Hollow. We were constantly being watched. No one liked us. Even the principal didn't like me at first. These communities were set in their ways, and they didn't want any "outsiders" ruining their perfect little lives. And they just didn't like the group home. They'd had past experiences where group-home kids had been awful, acted up, flirted, harassed a girl, things like that.

All the group-home kids had their own groups of friends at school—not the popular kids but the misfits. The popular kids looked at us like we were trash. People looked at me like I was a murderer. This one girl actually asked me what I was in the group home for, and I told her I'd murdered someone. She believed it. I thought, *Idiot, if I'd committed murder, why would I be in a group home?* Stupid kid. The teachers at Sleepy Hollow were okay. Some of them liked us; some didn't. Mr. Waldorf, the history teacher, liked us. He took care of us. He was a great teacher and really cared about us as people—didn't just look at us like convicts like everyone else.

I was depressed at that point. I wanted to kill myself almost every day. I used to drag my hands on the concrete just to bleed. Stupid shit. I needed attention. I needed someone to help me. I was calling out for help, and no one was answering, because I was broken. At that point, I was trying. But there was no passion behind it. I was just going through the motions because it felt like that's what I was supposed to do.

School let out at 2:12 p.m. After school, we'd all go back to the group home and have snack time. That was around three. Then homework time with the tutor ran from about three thirty to four thirty, something like that. The staff members didn't check that we actually did our homework. They didn't care if we did anything. We just had to sit there with the tutor. The tutors did care, though. I had some great tutors. Some would put me to sleep, but some were great. After time with the tutor, we had a break until dinner. I almost always used that time to go outside and shoot hoops with the guys. If we didn't use that time to play basketball, we'd sit inside and hang out and talk. Then we'd eat, do our assigned chores, and have free time. Any free time I had, I spent playing basketball. We'd go to the park, or we'd just go out back and hoop. We had some of the most epic games you can imagine. It was total street ball at its finest—fouling, elbowing, punching, grabbing, yelling, talking smack. We settled our differences out there. We fought. I broke my knee out there. That court saw it all. We were always back there grinding. The "court" was really just a hoop in the driveway. It was a long driveway that went all the way to the back of the house. At the end of the driveway was a three-car garage that was old as shit. That's where they kept the ugly-ass van they drove us around in. It was one of those big vans that fit twelve to fifteen people. We called it the Big Green Monster. Everywhere we went, we had to ride in that thing. It was notorious in the neighborhood. Everyone around town knew about "the group-home van."

Dinner was at five every night. One of the house chores was to help with dinner. No one liked that task. Then Tim joined the staff, and we got rid of that chore. He made all of our meals. After dinner, we cleaned up, and the staff checked everyone's chores. If you had done yours right, you could have free time before bed. Bedtimes were different based on your level. It was a system called ITL. I can't remember what that stood for. It was some sort of behavior program. If you had a certain status, you had to go to bed at eight. If you were well behaved and at a higher level, you could go to bed at nine thirty. I was a fairly good kid, so I had a nine-thirty bedtime. It wasn't really bedtime—just a time when you had to be in your room for the night. If you had a cool roommate, you could stay up as long as you wanted, as long as you stayed in your room. You could leave only to go to the bathroom. Sometimes we would sneak out and do "missions"—like steal food, run around outside, and fuck with each other and the staff members.

There were cliques in the house, but I fit in with everybody. For some reason everybody liked me. Not everyone got along with each other. We didn't all see eye to eye, but if there were any issues with outsiders, we were all together. If someone picked on a kid in our presence, we stuck up for him. We were a united front. There were certain times when you couldn't stand up for each other. You had to choose between your own path and someone else's. That happened once with me and my friend Squeak. He was jumped by three white kids—racist, dirtbag white kids taught to hate black people. They jumped him, and I knew if I got involved, I'd probably lose the fight and end up somewhere worse than the group home. Or I could stand there and look like a pansy and save myself—finish out my time at the group home and slowly inch toward a better existence. I chose to stand there. That decision both saved me and hurt me. It hurt me because I felt weak. I watched my man get destroyed. They were pounding his face into the locker. But I knew that if I went in, it would be over for me. Something told me that if I got involved, it was over. I'd never be shit. So I didn't. I stood there and watched him get his ass beaten. I watched the principal slam him into the locker. The guidance counselor grabbed me and pulled me into his office. I still don't know why. I didn't do anything. I didn't get in trouble, though. Then they shipped Squeak off to Bristol.

That was every week in the group home. Someone was there, and then they weren't. Their behavior was bad, the group home had had enough of them, and they were gone. So you had people you'd created friendships with and become close with, whether you liked them or not. You slept with them, ate with them, watched TV with them. You knew everything about them—their likes, their dislikes, if their home visit went okay, what was going on with their court case. Everything. Then one day they were gone. That was it. That was the most painful part of the group home.

When my buddy Darryl left, I was lost. He had been such a good friend. We were roommates. His chill demeanor complemented mine. He was such a chill dude. He had wanted to stay for his senior year, but he didn't get the chance. It was devastating. There was a loyalty, a bond, between us. We all went through the same shit. But the town hated us. Everybody hated us. That's why we were at the group home.

Aaron hung in there through it all. He never doubted. He saw something in me that no one else saw. Slowly, the staff kept working on me. They were patient and understanding. I was so angry, but they knew I had so much potential. On my good days, I was special. I could make anybody laugh. I could make the staff members' jobs so easy. I was a leader in the house. But on my bad days, I was awful. I tried to cut my wrists on concrete. I thought about suicide.

Jamie Hook was like the house mom. She was the nurturer. She took me under her wing. She was huge for me. She probably saved my life. I wanted to exit stage left. I thought, *It's been sixteen years. I've been through a lot. Why do I need to continue?* I thought about how to do it. Run in front of a car? Well, that might not work. I might just end up paralyzed. I couldn't get my hands on a gun. Knife? *Better hit the right organ*, I told myself. *Otherwise, you're stuck in a mental hospital where they watch you eat, shit, and sleep. Fuck that.* So I would just tell myself, *One more day, one more day, one more day.* I cut my wrists on concrete or rocks outside. I was crying for attention. I needed someone to pay attention to me because I was suffering. Jamie got me through everything. I was really depressed, and she would put me in check or give me the love I needed. She saved me. She really cared. She took me to get my hair cut. She bought me clothes and sneakers. When the new Jordan 17s came out, I was short around thirty dollars. Jaime just said, "Here you go," and gave me the thirty dollars. She didn't even think twice about it.

Then Jay came onto the scene. I hated him the first time I met him. He came to the house to visit before he started his job there. I took one look at him and said, "Who the fuck do you think you are, walking around this house like you own it? You don't even fucking work here." But he ended up becoming kind of like an older brother. Jay was maybe the most influential guy in my life. He taught me how to treat women and appreciate the simple things—like the bread on your sandwich, the mustard, the tomato. He came from the hood in New Jersey. He'd had a really rough life—gotten his ass beaten, his lunch money taken. He'd fought people. I wouldn't want to mess with him. He brought that mentality, the swagger, but also the perspective of "take care of your business, and appreciate the small things." He taught me how to dress, how to walk, how to talk. He taught me about the Gap and about how to talk to women. He taught me to build my wardrobe by buying one new shirt each time I got paid. He taught me about basketball. I had always played, and I had always loved the sport, but things really took off with him. When he got fired, I was hurt. He had said something wrong to one of the guys or something. I'm not totally sure, to be honest. But I was devastated without him. He was my guy, one of the best dudes I've ever met.

Dan was another staff member who took me under his wing. He was a short guy, but he could fuck shit up. I think he's a sheriff now. All these guys were tough, man, I tell you. They could all wipe the floor with me. I was built, but these guys could destroy me. Dan used to take me weightlifting, and we would joke around. We loved boy bands, so we'd play Backstreet Boys and N*Sync in the car on the way to lift weights. He got me into lifting weights.

It felt great living in the group home and not having parents. I felt a lot freer. The staff members were kind of like my parents, but at the end of the day, they weren't. To a certain extent, we all loved each other. But ultimately, everyone was just worried about themselves. The staff members weren't your parents. They went home at the end of the night. The guys all studied the staff members. We knew their schedules, when they would check on us, and when we could get away with fighting and stealing. My goal in the group home was just to survive—to get out and make it through. I learned a lot of lessons in the group home. There was pain, suffering, and happiness, all of it.

23

Brothers

IT WASN'T ALL BAD AT VALLEY VIEW. THERE WERE A LOT OF REALLY good times. We rocked that place. We lived hard. We rooted for each other when someone brought home a girl, then got mad together when it didn't work out with that girl. We were brothers. We were all lost. Aiden was weird, Toby had OCD, and Jordan was neat. Tommy was huge. He was trash on the court but would go to bat for you at any time. We talked about everything together. We had eating contests.

One of the guys I was in there with was Kevin, who changed my life. I called him "the Bodyguard." Back then, I was attracting a lot of negative attention at Sleepy Hollow. Christina Stedman's brother didn't like me for some reason. He wanted to beat my ass. When Kevin arrived, he protected me from everything. There were a few kids who wanted to get after me, but Kevin had my back. No one could beat him. Kevin was protective of me and wouldn't let anyone beat on me. One time, these two dudes were messing with me after class. I was handling it, I thought. But Kevin came up and took one dude in one hand and one in the other, slammed them into the lockers, and went to town—Kevin the Protector. When I broke my knee on the basketball court, Kevin made sure I didn't move and sat there with me. Good dude.

The group home was like one really big, fucked-up vacation. And the fights. My god. We could've had a reality show with all the crap that went on in that house. We fought over everything. We used to have full-house brawls for fun, using regular household items as weapons—belts, hangers, pencils, pens, boom boxes, anything we could get your hands on, even batteries in socks. It didn't matter what was available. We just went to town. I don't know how the group home's staff didn't hear these brawls. They were loud. I got hit with a hanger once.

I used to tell my buddy Harry to just hit me. I needed something to release the pain. I needed to focus on something. So he would hit me until it really hurt. I don't know why I was so sick. I was just in so much pain and hated everything so much. I just didn't see a way out. I thought I wasn't going amount to anything in life, so why would I care if I got hit? I got addicted to the pain. I wanted Harry to hit me with a broomstick, and he did. He'd get the broomstick and hit me over the back with it. And I felt like that's what I deserved. I was so used to getting hit that somehow in my sick mind I needed to feel hurt and pain. That's all I knew. Gina used to crack me so fucking hard, man, every day. I can still feel it. My first foster family hit me. Then Karen and Phil beat me. I was just so used to getting hit. Violence was the only thing I knew. I needed the pain. Harry would crack me on the back with the broom, and I'd tell him to keep going until I couldn't take it anymore. There were times I'd get hit so hard I couldn't move. I just wanted to see how far I could push it. I was so lost in my own head. That went on for a while. One day, Harry tried to hit me on the back, but he missed and cracked me in the knee instead. I turned into the Hulk on him. I grabbed this little guy, threw him against the wall, and started choking him. I wanted to release all the anger I'd been holding inside for years. I wanted to kill him. I was picturing my mom and Big Mike and Karen and Phil, and I just wanted to choke his fucking neck. But something told me to let go. So I did. Sorry, Harry. I didn't mean to fuck you up. You kind of deserved it, though.

There was so much drama in the house. We used to have food raids too, where we'd sneak food. I stole six pumpkin pies from the fridge once. I took them upstairs and sold them to the guys. Everyone in the group home got an allowance. If you did all your chores, you'd get ten dollars a week. I got money from the state too—a whopping forty-five dollars per month, I think. Sometimes I spent it on an extra lunch. But I also bought a DMX CD and shell-toe shoes, and I got my hair cut to impress girls. I thought I was so cool with that fresh fade. I thought all the girls would want me. They didn't.

Every day felt like forever in the group home. I was never getting anywhere. But I got addicted to it. I loved it and hated it at the same time. There was nothing like coming home and knowing that eleven people you were really close to were there waiting for you—your brothers. It was way better than Karen and Phil's, that's for damn sure.

24

Fetal Alcohol Syndrome

THE GROUP HOME SAVED ME FROM DEATH, WITHOUT A DOUBT. I WAS suicidal in the group home, but the staff members stayed with me the whole way. They never gave up. They didn't like the tasks they had to carry out—like when Karen had me tested for fetal alcohol syndrome when I was sixteen. She thought I looked retarded and said I had characteristics of down syndrome or fetal alcohol syndrome. She brought up the fact that my mom probably had been drunk or high or both when she was pregnant with me. So she asked the courts to have me tested. I was sixteen years old, and my own mom was having me tested for retardation. That was an entirely different type of humiliation from what I'd ever experienced before. That one hurt. I remember the group home staff member who took me for the test—Melinda, I think, a redhead. She was an awesome human being, so nice. She called me into the office and said, "You have a doctor's appointment." I said, "For what?" and she handed me the paper with the info about the appointment. I looked it over and figured it out before Melinda had a chance to say much. I asked her, "My mom thinks I'm retarded?" She answered, "Look, I just have to do what they tell me to do. I don't like this. You know I like you a lot, but I have to do what I'm told."

Melinda drove me up to Millfield for my exam. The drive took about an hour and a half. I think it was Millfield at least. I wasn't paying attention. I was too upset to care. I was so distraught that I sat in the back seat and cried the whole way there. Usually, I'd sit in the front, but I was such a wreck that I just wanted to sit in the back and cry. I always tried to be tough, but I just couldn't do it that time. I sobbed the entire car ride. I felt so upset that my own mom would do this to me, so humiliated that I had to go through with it. All I could do was cry. Melinda tried to cheer me up the whole time. She said we could get fast food after the appointment. "We'll get burgers after, and you don't need to go back to school today. You can have the rest of the day off." But it wasn't working. I was miserable. When we got there, I refused to get out of the car. Melinda had to beg me to get out of the car. She understood it was bullshit, but she had to do her job. It wasn't her fault.

Melinda took me inside the center, and I was called into a room with an older lady. She was a heavyset woman with gray hair and glasses, wearing a purple shirt. She was very friendly and welcomed me in. "Hi, Chris. How are you?" she said. After a few other niceties, she asked me a series of humiliating questions. She asked me to play with blocks to see if I could build a block tower. I literally had to put four blocks on top of each other—at sixteen years old! Then she did one of those stupid tests where the tester tells you to "point to a tree," and you're supposed to point to the picture of the tree. She asked me about sports and if there were any sports that I liked. I told her I played soccer, ran track and field, and liked basketball. She asked, "When you play basketball, do you actually get any of the balls in the basket?"— basically implying that I was disabled and couldn't make a jump shot. I looked at her and snapped back, "We can go to a court right now and find out. Let's go—let's find a park, and I'll show you." I was good at basketball, or decent anyway. I was athletic. And this idiot thought she would question my skill. Psh. Get outta here with that bullshit.

I've dealt with a lot of bullshit during my time on earth, but that was one of the most humiliating experiences of my life. Something about my "mom" accusing me of being retarded and making me build block towers at age sixteen really fucked me up. I'll never forgive her for that one.

25

Basketball

I STARTED REALLY LOVING BASKETBALL AROUND SIXTH GRADE. I played soccer, but I didn't get along with anybody because of my past. And I didn't like being told what to do. I still don't. Soccer was supposed to be my sport, but it wasn't. I wanted to be a pro athlete when I was a kid. I loved playing basketball more than anything. I wanted to play in the NBA. I wanted to make millions of dollars. I wanted to have everything. My basketball dreams were taken away due to the shit Karen and Phil put me through. I practiced every day to make the varsity basketball team in school, but it was all for nothing. I got locked up—basketball career over. I never had a chance. Never. And I got cut from the team at Sleepy Hollow. Why? Because the coach's son was really better than me? Yeah, okay, sure he was. I couldn't even make varsity. I wanted to play varsity basketball, and I never got the chance. Man, it sucked. My actions from all the shit that had happened cost me any sense of normal life. The only thing I wanted in high school was to play varsity basketball. It was my dream to play and have everyone cheer for me. I wanted to be the coolest person in the school. I wanted to go to all the parties. I wanted the teachers to just give me A's because I was able to bounce a ball. That was the dream.

I love basketball, man. That game saved my life. I mean, you can see it in my clothes even now. I wear something Jordan brand every day. I had nothing without the game. I just thought I was a worthless piece of shit, thanks to Karen and Phil constantly tearing me down and making me think that way. With basketball, though, I felt like I was somebody. And I was. When I went to parks, I would play my heart out. By the time we were done, everyone knew who that skinny white kid on the court was. I would make it rain out there. If I was hot, good luck! Those days are gone, but people will tell you about them. I might not have made the NBA or been great, but I could play. And the game saved me. I was able to focus on something that took me away from the bullshit that was going on with Karen and Phil or in school or in the group home. Everything just faded away when I played basketball. My past, my present, my struggles—none of it mattered on the court.

When I lived in the group home, I had nothing but basketball. Once I got my hoop, basketball was all I cared about. I really thought I could make the NBA. It's crazy—I actually thought I could make the NBA. Those guys are six feet eight and 260 pounds. They run like fucking deer. I have the utmost respect for them. So many of those players really care about the world—building schools and donating money and giving hope to kids. That's what I wanted to be. But I was robbed of my chance.

When I was going through all my shit, there were a few basketball players who kept me going. They're the reasons I'm here today. When I was four or five, I got a stopwatch with this one basketball player on it. He was sticking his tongue out, and he looked so cool. I used to see clips of this guy on TV, and everything he did was just amazing—the way he walked, the way he talked, the way he played the game, the way he sat. Very few people really captured my attention like he did. He was something I had never seen and I knew I was never going to see. He was phenomenal. For someone to be that good at what they do—man, think about that. Think about the hours of sweat, preparation, and training. That's what I liked most about him. His determination helped me because I was facing some hard shit. I was getting my ass beaten all the time. I was going through mental warfare and getting killed every day for everything I did. His mentality was *Who cares? Go hard every play, every day.* And I did. I think when he retired, I lost that. I kind of lost that mentality. I was really down. I just didn't care. I figured I'd done enough. None of this shit made sense. The world didn't make sense. I started asking myself, *What's the fucking point?* And I didn't feel like I had one. I didn't have a reason.

What this guy was able to do was give me an outlet when I had nothing—no friends, no family. I saw my sisters once in a blue moon. I never saw anybody else. I was getting crushed in every area. Every foster home was the same bullshit. Everything was hell. I was miserable. But he was always there. He would do something so amazing on the court that it would make me forget that I was living in hell. No one wanted me, and no one liked me, but he made me forget about all that. In my life, just like in the bathtub at Gina's, I won't stay down. Whenever I was smacked, I got up. And I got that from my favorite basketball player—because no matter what you did to him, he gave you game 7 mentality every time. He had a mentality that resonated with me early on, one that said, "I'm not going to lose without a fight." You might knock me out, you might destroy me, but until I can't breathe, I'm gonna keep going. And that's how I got through it. Even through depression, I tried to be the best I could. It's a miracle I'm not locked up or dead or completely a wreck. Glory goes to God. But basketball helped, because I was able to focus on something. That player is a hero in my book. He's a legend. My life was a wreck. I was mean. I attacked everyone and everything that came near me. But I'm not that person anymore. My favorite basketball player—and in my eyes, the greatest basketball player of all time—definitely saved my life.

26

Graduation

THE WEEKEND BEFORE MY HIGH SCHOOL GRADUATION, PHIL AND Karen threw me a party at their house. I wasn't allowed to go inside except to use the bathroom. Karen was still scared of me, so I was only allowed to celebrate outside in the yard. It was a really fun party, though. They got me a cake, and there was food for days. We had one of those kiddie pools from Walmart, along with the big aboveground pool they had in the yard. All my favorite aunts were there. I won two awards—"Most Valuable Player" on the volleyball team and "Most Improved" athlete over varsity career. I was the only one at school to win the second award. It felt really special.

Graduation was one of the loneliest moments for me. I had just graduated from Sleepy Hollow, one of the worst high schools in New York. My first high school, Woodrow Roosevelt, was one of the best. Both schools hated me because of my issues, but whatever. I was standing there, and I thought, *This is it. This is the end of this chapter. I'm never gonna see these people again.* I didn't really see any of my high school classmates after that day. And seeing group-home kids was even more rare. I don't even know if they're all alive. A lot of them went on to be locked up. It's a statistics game. Adults told us that most of us wouldn't make shit of ourselves, that we'd just be in the system for the rest of our lives, that we were fucking criminals.

So we just kind of took it and figured they must be right. If they didn't believe in me, I didn't believe in me, so fuck it. I assumed I'd just be a dope dealer. Or maybe I'd rob people. We all had potential, except for the ones who really murdered people. The public saw us all as a cancer or threat. Maybe on some levels we were, but we just needed the right direction. I'm proof of that. When I got to Valley View, I just wanted to fight everybody and everything, and I just didn't care. I cared enough to remain there. I didn't want to go to Bristol. But I had a lot of incidents, like when I chased a staff member with a brick, probably because she told me to do chores. Stupid shit.

After graduation, I went back to the group home and packed up my stuff. That was June 29. My exit date was July 2. That date came, and I said goodbye to everybody. I tried to keep a straight face. This place was all I'd known for years. Valley View was it. It was me. I was a big part of that house. We had a lot of great days in that house. And it was over.

In came the head of Bristol, Bruce Addison, because the group home was affiliated with Bristol. He looked at me and said, "Get your feet off the fucking table." I looked back at him and said, "Fuck you. Make me get my feet off the table." He was like "What did you say?" And I said, "My release date is today. What are you gonna do? What?" He knew he couldn't do a fucking thing. It was so satisfying.

When you're locked up, the staff members bug you. They're nice enough but annoying. They had stupid policies that didn't make any sense. The policies didn't put the kids' safety or well-being or mental health first. Bruce Addison was one of those people who just cared about his paychecks. He didn't care about the kids. He got paid a lot of money. He had a fancy degree, and he was fat; he clearly ate a lot. He would just pick us apart for every little thing. So that was my one chance to tell him, basically, *Fuck you. You're not better than me. I beat you. I beat the system. I beat all these fucking odds. I beat*

Gina. I beat Karen and Phil. I fucking made it. That was the best feeling. I felt so liberated.

As I was driven away from the group home for the last time, I was thinking, *Yeah, I made it to eighteen.* People had said I wouldn't make it to eighteen. They had said I wouldn't graduate high school, and I had. I'd beaten the odds. It was crazy.

The group home staff dropped me off at my grandpa's house on Blueberry Drive. They dumped me on the lawn, threw my shit on the lawn after me, and said, "Peace. Have a good life. See ya never." And that was it.

27

Grampy's

GETTING TO GRAMPY'S WAS SUCH A LOW EXPERIENCE. I DIDN'T know what to do. In the group home, they told you everything. They told you when to eat, when to sleep, and everything you needed to do at all times. The tutors practically did your homework for you. You just had to be a physical being to do well. Just show up, and you'd be fine. A lot of kids couldn't even do that. But I could. So when I got to Grampy's, I had no idea what to do.

Grampy was Phil's stepdad. He was a brainiac, one of the smartest people you'd ever meet. He helped build computers all around the world and went to Rensselaer Polytechnic Institute, one of the top colleges in New York State. Super chill dude—kind of weird, but always a good dude. I stayed in his basement unit, which had everything—a bedroom, a living room, a private entrance off to the side, and a bathroom. That's where I had to stay because I wasn't allowed to go home to Karen and Phil's. Staying at Grampy's place was weird. He got up at five every morning. I snuck out of the house every night to go to Denny's and hang out with girls. This time was my first taste of freedom in forever. I had things I wanted to do. And he kept trying to tell me to get a job.

One of the first things I did was get a YMCA membership so I could play basketball. I was living the life. If I wasn't playing basketball, I was running. If I wasn't running, I was at the Y playing basketball. I hung out with Meg and Charlie a lot. We were just friends. We would go out and eat and hang out and talk and laugh. I felt like such a badass because I was staying out late. Lights-out at the group home had been 9:30 p.m.

Grampy made me get a job, but I got fired. I didn't want to work at a gas station. I'd just gotten my freedom. Fuck that. It was a pretty decent summer, though. Then I was off to college.

28

Walnut Creek

I WAS ONE OF ONLY TWO KIDS FROM THE GROUP HOME TO GO TO college. I went to Walnut Creek Community College. I didn't understand the college life at first. But I picked it up pretty quickly. I went to basically the only community college that had dorms. I needed somewhere to live since I couldn't go back to Karen and Phil's. I wasn't a great student. I just really didn't like school. It didn't speak to me. If it speaks to you, I commend you. The diligence and hard work it takes to complete a degree are really impressive. But it just wasn't for me. I was lost. I would go to class and think, *What is the point of this?* Even now, if I don't see the point in something, I won't do it.

I looked like a thug, wearing my baggy pants and a jersey. I didn't fit in. While at college, I met Franklin, who's now my best friend. My dorm room was right next to his, and I used to hear him banging on the walls because he was such a passionate sports fan. I would bang on the walls back, and we became friends. We're best friends to this day. The year I spent at Walnut Creek was one of the best years of my life, though not from an academic standpoint. I think I finished the second semester with a 0.9 GPA. But man, we had some good times. Every night was an adventure. Franklin had my back like you wouldn't believe.

I played Division III lacrosse. I walked onto the team. I used to play basketball, and I was decent at it. I probably could've made the team. The lacrosse coach came by one day while I was scrimmaging and said, "Hey, what are you up to this spring?" I asked, "What do you mean?" Again, he asked, "What are you up to?" I told him I worked in the cage—that's where people could go to get a basketball or a volleyball so they could play. But other than that, I wasn't doing anything. He couldn't believe it. "You're not on a team?" he asked. I said no. I told him I wanted to do track, but I wasn't fast enough. "Bullshit!" he told me. "I coach the lacrosse team, and I need you on the team." I was like "Coach, I only played lacrosse for like two weeks in high school." He asked, "Can you run? Are you fast? Are you agile?" I could, I could, and I was. Back then I could fly. I was an elite athlete. So he told me to come out and give it a shot.

I got to the field and was shocked at what a physical game lacrosse was. There were times I'd get hit by someone running what felt like ninety miles an hour. During one of my first practices, I tried to go down for a low ball, but I didn't get low enough or drop my head, and this kid obliterated me. I don't remember shit. I just remember hitting the ground, my head spinning, and that was it. I definitely had a couple concussions. Other than being a scrub on the bench, it wasn't bad at all.

My first week at WCCC, I met Claire, who I thought was the girl of my dreams. I have nothing but respect for her. It didn't work out, but she was extremely helpful for me. She was patient and understanding and helped me through a lot of my issues. She got the ball rolling and helped me get to where I am now. She'd always tell me, "You can't let your past cripple you." Because that's what it would do. Anytime anything good would happen, I'd feel like shit and like I didn't deserve it. That carried on well into my adult life. When you go through what I went through as a kid, it has lasting effects. You might try to move on, but you can't accept anything, not winning or losing or anything. You're just miserable in your own head. You're supposed to celebrate when you win something. But I didn't think that way. Now I'm able to realize that it's okay to celebrate the wins. I won. It took me a while to realize it. But I beat the system. I broke it. I wasn't supposed to be here, but I am. So you can be here too.

I was at Walnut Creek for a year. I made some bad financial decisions and couldn't afford to go back. I thought I was going to move to Virginia. I went there once and thought it was cool and wanted to live there. Claire and I were going to live there together, but her mom convinced us to move into her trailer with her. We ended up staying in the trailer and never made it to Virginia. It wasn't in the cards. I kind of wandered around there. I took some minimum-wage jobs while we all lived in Claire's mom's trailer. Claire and I eventually broke up. I was too angry. So she kicked me out, and I had to move back home with Karen.

29

Home Again

KAREN AND PHIL WERE DIVORCED AT THAT POINT. HE COULDN'T put up with her anymore. It's honestly amazing that he lasted as long as he did. He had moved out and was living in an apartment. It was small. And I wanted to go home, to the big house. I called Karen on the phone first. I said, "Look, I have nowhere to go. I don't want to be in this situation. But I got dumped. I need a place to go, and you're it." The person I had wanted to marry didn't want to be with me anymore. She couldn't have looked any more disinterested in me. I'll never forget that. Karen said I could move in. I told her I just wanted to be left alone. I didn't want to do her stupid chores. I just needed a little time to get my head out of my ass and figure out what to do. She was surprisingly okay with that.

I moved in and didn't even have a bedroom. I was sleeping in the living room, on the couch. That was the first strike. At first, I was commuting two hours to Kingston, New York, to work at Office Depot for $7/hour. Then I got two jobs—Macy's and Piercing Pagoda. I was biding time really. I was supposed to move into the apartment at Aunt Anne's. Aunt Anne had offered me an apartment, but I didn't want to impose. For some reason I thought that moving in was imposing, because I thought I wasn't worthy. I was waiting to see if any other opportunities came along. Aunt Anne's was kind of my last resort.

Things got off to a decent start at Karen's, then they started to fall apart, like they always did. Karen got really weird. She told me she needed me to pay rent. She wanted to charge me $400–500/ month to live at my own house. That was strike two. I was thinking, *I'm never going to get out of here if I can't save.* The whole point was to save. And she was trying to charge me to live in my own house? I couldn't believe it. She also said I couldn't eat the food from my own fridge. She would literally yell at me for eating food. Strike three.

Eventually, it all came to a head. She wanted her money, and I was tired of paying her. I wanted sneakers. I'd been saving everything and just wanted to treat myself. But she got really agitated. She was like "Look, I need that money." And it just spiraled into a big argument. I said something like "How's it feel to be in your sixties and still freeloading off of your ex?" and she said, "Likewise, how's it feel to be your age and freeloading off your mom?" Freeloading? Can you believe it? I had to remind her, "I have two fucking jobs. You have two master's degrees and haven't had a job in twenty years. You're a bum." She told me I had two weeks to leave, or she'd kick me out. So I told her I'd be out in two days. And I was.

30

GTO Girl

I MET A FRIEND ON THE INTERNET, IN AN AOL CHAT ROOM. Remember those? Everyone loved an AOL chat room. The chat room was called "under21." I used to go into chat rooms and talk shit about everyone just to get a rise out of them. It was entertaining for me. I never thought I'd meet these people, so what did I care? But one day, someone named GTO Girl messaged me and asked if we could chat. I figured, *Fuck it—why not?* If it sucked, I would just talk shit to her and entertain myself. It ended up being a decent chat. And it just took off from there. Her real name was Tammy. She lived in Chicago (well, the suburbs of Chicago). She sent me a photo of herself. I wasn't happy with what I saw, but she offered to head to New York and pick me up and take me away from Karen's, so I didn't care.

She said, "Look, I'm driving to get you. It'll be sixteen hours." She told me what time she'd pick me up. I was skeptical at first, but I figured, why not? It sounded better than staying at Karen's. I took a leap of faith. I had $250 in my pocket and decided to trust this random stranger from the internet. For some reason it worked. And I still don't know how.

Tammy drove to a Walmart parking lot about a mile away from Karen's house, and I drove to meet her there. I didn't want her picking me up at Karen's because I didn't want Karen to know I was leaving. I didn't want to say goodbye or pay her rent. I just wanted her to see that I was gone.

Tammy came to pick me up in a two-door sedan. She had a friend in the passenger seat. They were both four hundred to five hundred pounds. I had to sit in the back seat with her friend Amy, who couldn't go ten seconds without a cigarette. My seat was behind Tammy, so I had no legroom. But I ultimately had to decide if I wanted to cram into that car and go for a better life away from Karen or stay with Karen and crawl back with my tail between my legs and pay rent for a house I basically had helped build. So I got in the car with two bags. I had brought three, but only two fit. I left the other one in my Dodge Neon in the Walmart parking lot. That car stayed in the parking lot for something like eight months after I left.

We all started talking and hit it off right away. I put them at ease. They bought me Burger King. We got to Chicago and went right to Tammy's apartment. She had a roommate, some girl named Sarah. Sarah didn't like that I was staying there. Sometimes I slept on the futon with Tammy, but it wasn't really comfortable for two people. So I slept on the couch a lot. I didn't have to worry about anything at first. Tammy took care of everything. She didn't have a job, but her parents helped with everything. She was in school at a local community college, but she barely went. She was a different soul—lost in a lot of areas but really beautiful in other areas. She could be the nicest person in the world if she wanted to be. But she could also be an asshole if she wanted to be. We didn't officially date right away. We were just friends for the first year or so. To be honest, I couldn't see myself dating her because she was fat. I know it sounds harsh, but I'm just trying to be as honest as possible. I had been through a lot of pain in my life, and I thought she would die young because of her weight. She would die young, and she couldn't have kids. That just sounded like a no-win situation to me. I knew I wouldn't be happy with her long-term. But we had some good times. We hung out all the time. We went shopping, watched TV, and hung out with her family. I became close friends with some of her siblings. I just couldn't be free with her.

We had a lot of issues. Things got physical. We said a lot of mean shit to each other. She said I was a mistake—told me Gina should've drowned me. In her defense, I said a lot of mean things to her too. It wasn't healthy. We just didn't click. We forced it. We wanted it to work, but it just didn't. I couldn't get past certain things with her. She's a beautiful person, she is, but I just couldn't do it anymore. We ended up getting engaged after eight years together, because I thought that was what everyone expected. I thought I wouldn't be able to find anyone better. So I settled. I knew before the wedding that we weren't meant to be. But I felt like I couldn't get out of it, so we went through with it. Her parents went on our honeymoon with us, if you could even call it a honeymoon. I just wasn't ever really satisfied with where I was. I didn't want to live in the suburbs of Illinois. Tammy refused to move farther than fifteen minutes from her parents' house. I didn't want to have to babysit her and take care of her issues. I wanted to be free. I wanted to go for long walks on the beach and have a girl who could keep up with me and go on adventures. I needed to fulfill my creativity. I felt stifled with Tammy. The biggest issue was her attitude. She didn't want to put in any effort or try at all, at weight loss or at life. It just got to me. She promised that things would change and she would take her health seriously, but it never happened.

One day we got into a little scuffle, and I shoved her. I didn't mean to shove her. I really didn't. But she slipped on something and crashed into the bathtub. It scared the shit out of me. I hadn't expected that to happen. I didn't think I was that strong. I didn't think it would be that impactful. I just thought I would send a message—that she needed to back off. I didn't think I would hurt her. Ever since then, I've been terrified to be near people if I'm angry. I'm under control, but I just walk away. That moment woke me up to how violent I was. I used to let my hands do the talking instead of my words. Because of my past and my childhood, I didn't know how to process things. I processed things through anger, instead of being diplomatic or talking through issues. So I ended up having conflict issues, issues with holding down a job, and issues with getting physical, like the situation with her. I learned how to control it. I guess I have Tammy to thank for that.

There were times I would look at her and just didn't like her. We had a lot of ups and downs. Her family was great, though. She has one of the best families ever. I feel bad for her. I can't imagine having to deal with what she dealt with every single day. To be five feet six and 465 pounds and have people be so mean—I used to feel so empty inside and heartbroken at how people would treat her. Some of the things people would say were unacceptable. I used to have to sit there and listen to people call her names, and it was devastating. Every time it happened, I watched her lose a piece of herself inside. And every time, I'd have to calm her down and let her know that it wasn't true and I loved her. I did love her, just as a person, not a wife. I needed to be free. I needed a girl who could let me be myself and not tell me to be something I wasn't and someone who could help me on my journey to figure out what I was here to do. Tammy couldn't do it. We barely hung out toward the end. She was never home. She basically lived at home in the suburbs with her parents for a solid year before we got married and left me alone in our apartment. I hung in there a long time, though. I gave her everything I had. But I was burned out. I wasn't the same anymore. It was time for me to close that chapter and head out. So after only three months of marriage, I told Tammy I wanted a divorce. I'm sure her family hates me now, but that's okay. I really wish them well. They are a great family.

31

Border Patrol

WHEN I FIRST MOVED TO CHICAGO, I WAS LOST. TAMMY LET ME hang out without a job for a few years, but I knew I had to contribute eventually. The problem was I didn't know what to do. I had a really spotty job history and wasn't really good at anything. I worked at Macy's for a few months, but I quit when they wouldn't let me take a day off to watch a Miami Hurricanes football game. I was an idiot. I bounced around from retail gigs to hotel security jobs and finally landed a job as a security guard at a mall on Michigan Avenue. Ralph saw my résumé and my attitude, but he didn't care. He took a chance on me. I will be forever grateful to him for that. He became like a father to me. I looked up to him, listened to him, and cared about him. I hated my job, but I loved working with Ralph. Plus, it was a steady income and easy work, so I stuck it out. I really wanted to be a Border Patrol officer. The agency was based in Arizona, but I didn't care. I thought it was a prestigious career that people respected. I would be doing something that had meaning. That's what the agency wanted you to think. They tried to make it sound like a noble career, but in reality, they just wanted to pay people something like $32,000 a year to stand in the desert and have angry motherfuckers throw rocks at them all day. For all the shit the agents have to put up with, their salary needs to be bumped up to at least twice that amount.

And were there even stock options? Or any other benefits that would make that job worth it? That shit is crazy.

I made it through a few rounds of interviews but shit the bed at the lie detector test. I didn't lie. I just got nervous and said too much. The officer interviewing me tried to mess with me. I know what he fucking did. He got inside my head and dangled the bait, and I took it. I knew after I took the bait that it was over. I knew it. It was a game. He was trying to rile me up to get me to say something I didn't want to say, and that's what happened. I told him about the Tammy situation, how I had shoved her, and her head smacked against the wall, and she fell into the tub. And he said something like "Whoa, man! You're a big guy—you can't be doing things like that!" I knew then that it was over.

The whole way back home after the interview, I kept thinking, *Oh my god, I have to go back to being a fucking mall cop. That's what I'm gonna be doing. I have to go back to making $10 an hour to tell people not to run in the fucking building.* Like, who cares if somebody runs in the building? I never understood security guards. We were all like "Okay, we're just gonna stand here and look around. You have to follow the rules. No, don't do that. I can't do anything about it if you do. But just don't do it. Or I'm gonna call somebody who can do something about it." That's what I was doing for a living, instead of Border Patrol. I felt like such a failure.

As I headed back home, I thought about killing myself. I thought, *How am I gonna do it? I could jump off a bridge—that would probably be pretty quick.* I felt like I shouldn't even go home because I was such a fucking embarrassment. Then I got to the bridge and thought, *I don't know. It's a little cold. I don't think I want to kill myself today. I'll just get on the train and get back to my sucky life.* And I did. I went back to my shitty fucking life as a mall security guard, watching people live their lives, watching people buy useless items they didn't need. People would go into Nordstrom with a Balenciaga bag, buy a new bag, and walk out with two bags. They already had one. Why did they need two? It was so greedy. But I was jealous. I wanted to be able to shop like that too.

After the Border Patrol attempt, I started training to be a private security guard with Gavin DeBecker. It was a long shot. I think something like two out of every thousand applicants got accepted to Gavin DeBecker's program. I did well and thought I was going to get hired. I ran a 6:51 mile, which was the fastest mile I had ever run. I think I had run a mile in the six-minute range only one other time. But the other guys ran closer to five-minute miles. I didn't stand a chance.

When I failed at Gavin DeBecker, I decided I wanted to be a police officer with the Rockford Police Department. At first, I thought, *You're gonna move to Rockford? Really? It's like three hours from Chicago.* But then I thought that maybe if I got hired, I could live in Chicago and travel to Rockford for work. I didn't know. I just knew I needed to get in somewhere. Those were my options. I mean, the economy was shit. I went to Lake in the Hills PD, which was hiring two officers, and they had something like four hundred people in the room. Four hundred people came to the fucking meeting. And they were only taking two. I got up mid-session and left. No way was I getting that.

The Rockford PD application process was fine. I had gained around ten pounds after Gavin DeBecker, and that slowed me down a bit. I sucked at distance running. I barely beat the thirteen-minute requirement for a mile and a half—barely. It was down to the last lap. I wasn't supposed to beat that. That's what I think. And don't get me started on the academic portion. I think I finished with maybe the lowest score ever. I didn't come close to getting the job in Rockford. I bombed. I killed the bench-press portion, though, as usual. It just wasn't enough to get the job.

After that, I didn't see the point of life anymore. I especially didn't see the point of working. I thought I was working so someone else at the top could live it up and have the best life and not give a shit about the people who got him there. That just seemed ass backwards. It seemed like everybody should have an equal share in their company's earnings. Okay, fine, the CEOs should have maybe a double share or triple share, or maybe even a quadruple share. But why should they get all the money while the hardworking people at the bottom didn't get any? I just thought, *Fuck that.* I didn't want to do that shit. Fuck it. If I could exit this world and just wait in purgatory and not cross over to heaven right away, then why wouldn't I do that? If I could have somewhere better than earth and not quite heaven, then cross over eventually, why not do it? Because I knew I'd be filled with instant regret. I always thought I'd get up there, and God would take me into her office and play me a video of all the amazing things I'd missed out on. Sometimes I didn't care. Other times, I thought, *Maybe I'll stick around and see if it gets better.* When I met Mallory, I was ready to give up. But boy, am I glad I didn't.

32

Mal

THIS WAS (AND IS) THE BEST CHAPTER OF MY LIFE, FOR SURE. I WAS
still working as a mall cop. I got to tell people not to run in the
hallways. Exciting stuff. I was at a point in my life where I was just
depressed. I felt like if I didn't have a real job by the time I turned
thirty, I'd probably kill myself. I just felt like I didn't have anything.
I hadn't gotten the Border Patrol job or the Rockford PD job or any
other job. I felt worthless. I thought I'd ride it out as long as I could,
but I made up my mind that eventually I was going to bow out, and
no one would notice. I was convinced I would end up killing myself,
and literally no one would care. Every day I'd think, *Maybe I'll kill
myself tomorrow.* But there was always something that kept me from
going through with it. *Potbelly has 10 percent off today, so I'll wait
until tomorrow.* Then tomorrow would come, and the Lakers would
have a game. So I'd say, *Okay, I'll watch the Lakers today and kill
myself tomorrow.* I used to go to the roof of the parking garage and
think about jumping. But every time I'd get close to the edge, I'd
think, *Well, what if it doesn't work and I just end up paralyzed?* and
put it off again. *Nah, I'll do it tomorrow.*

Then Mal showed up. I was standing at the front entrance one
day, feeling useless and beating myself up in my head, when I saw
this young woman going up the escalator. She was beautiful. The

first thing I noticed was her eyes. I was hooked from the start. Our eyes met, and there was an instant connection. I can't explain it. She smiled and said hello. She said hi to everyone. It didn't matter what job you had or what clothes you wore. She didn't care about that stuff. She was wearing red that first day. Her hair was straight. And when she looked at me, I was hooked. I just knew I had to get to know her. First, I had to figure out what store she worked in. I just couldn't believe she worked at the mall. She seemed way too good for the mall. She never acted it, though. She was always humble and talked to everyone. I walked around every floor that day and looked in each store as I walked by. I was trying not to be too obvious, but I had to find her. I found her on the second floor. Her name was Mallory, and she worked at Sunglass Hut.

I would walk by her store every day just to say hi. We formed a bond that way. We'd chat outside her store or in the food court on our breaks. Initially, I just wanted to be her friend. My self-esteem was beyond low. I just needed a buddy. I wanted to talk to her and have someone to kick it with. At that point, I was scheduled to marry Tammy in about a month, but I knew it wasn't going to work. I felt it. But I didn't want to throw away $30,000, so I just kept up with it. I didn't want to disappoint her family. I felt like I was too far in it to back out. Knowing what I know now, I wish I would have.

Mal was super sarcastic. I think that's why I was drawn to her initially. She was a challenge. One day, I told her I had plantar fasciitis in both feet, and she said, "That sucks," shrugged, and went back to reading her *RedEye* newspaper. She read that silly thing every morning. I didn't get any sympathy from her, which somehow made me like her even more. One thing led to another, and we formed a solid friendship. We tweeted at first. We were on Twitter nonstop. One day we were talking about exchanging phone numbers, and she said, "Well, get out your phone then." She was always pretty ballsy and a straight shooter. She was not into playing games. I liked that about her.

One of the first times we hung out was when she had to go to Macy's on State Street and asked if I wanted to go with her. How lame is that? She invited me to go with her to spend a gift card. But it was so fun. I remember how authentic and real she was and how warm I felt around her. I had never felt that with anybody. She treated me to my first Starbucks drink—a caramel Frappuccino, because I didn't like coffee. We laughed and shopped. She bought some stuff for her kitchen and a memory foam pillow. And by the end of that trip, I was connected to her in a way I couldn't explain. I wanted to spend every minute with her. I didn't want her to leave. I didn't want her to go home. And that's how I knew it was special. I couldn't wait to see her again.

We started hanging out more and more. We became insepara-ble. I'd go to her apartment in Rogers Park, and she would make turkey burgers, and we would watch *The Bachelor.* I pretended I wasn't into it, but honestly, *Bachelor* Monday was (and still is) one of my favorite days of the week. Mal's roommates were all awesome and didn't seem to mind that I hung out there a lot. I was also her "personal trainer." We would do half-assed workouts on the sidewalk outside her apartment. Really, we just goofed around and laughed the whole time. We became best friends. We flirted occasionally but never did anything beyond flirting. It was around that time that I broke it off with Tammy. It was hard. Divorce sucks. I really loved her family and was sad to say goodbye to them. But I don't regret it for a second—best decision I ever made.

After a few months of hanging out, Mal and I started dating. We went to Jaks Tavern in the West Loop to watch a Creighton basket-ball game. Back then, Jaks was the official Creighton bar where all the alumni in the area could go to watch the games. I had never felt a rush quite like that night before. It was like nothing else. I remem-ber that Mal told me I had to behave myself because I was going to be hanging out with her school friends at basketball night. My first thought was *Who are these nerds, and why can't we watch this game at a real bar?* They were great, though—so nice and welcoming. They never made me feel like less than them because I hadn't gone to a real college. I was always self-conscious of that. I thought I wouldn't fit in because I'd gone to community college. But it didn't matter with the Creighton crew. They were great. Mal and I drank two pitchers of Three Floyds Gumball Head and just had fun. When we kissed for the first time, it was the greatest moment ever. I felt alive. That was the first time I'd felt alive. I never say corny shit like this, but I really felt like life was breathed into me.

After Jaks, we went to a club in the Loop with some of my work friends. We danced and kissed and laughed. I took Mal home at the end of the night. She was beyond drunk and asked me to stay the night. I think she was too drunk to do anything physical. She just wanted me to keep her company. I told her I couldn't do that. She wasn't in her right frame of mind, and I wanted her to be fully aware when she made that decision. So I tucked her into bed and left. I really wanted to stay, but I wanted her to know I respected her and her space and had her best interests at heart.

A few days later, February 12, 2013, we went to Giordano's together for dinner. That's when Mal asked, "So are you my boyfriend now?" I said, "Yes, if you'll have me," and that was it. We were officially boyfriend and girlfriend. We've been together ever since. It hasn't been all sunshine and rainbows. We went through some growing pains. In the beginning, I was a wreck. I gave up everything to chase this girl, and I paid the price. I had no friends or family. My own family turned on me when I broke it off with Tammy. I gave up the farm for Mallory. But it was 100 percent worth it. I'd do it again in a heartbeat.

If I had to do it again, though, I'd like to skip the crappy apartment part. After I left Tammy, I moved into an apartment in a house around forty minutes from downtown. It might as well have been Wisconsin, it felt so far away. I called it Nick's house. Nick was one of the guys who lived there. It wasn't really his house, but he thought it was. He took over the entire house for himself. He was the only one who used the kitchen, and he was always cooking. He had racks of clothes lining the walls of the living room. I was stuffed in a little room on a mattress that wasn't mine. It had come with the place. I don't even want to think about who slept on it before me. There were seven or eight people in the house. The landlord and his mom lived upstairs, Nick and one other dude and I were on the main floor, and there were a few people in the basement unit. It was a mess. There were pubic hairs everywhere. It was nasty. But it was $400/month, and I didn't have anywhere else to go. Around that time, Mal moved into a new apartment in a different neighborhood. I stayed there most nights, but her new roommates said I stayed too much. They weren't very nice. I tried to stay out of their way as best as I could. I even gave them some money toward rent to make up for any trouble I caused. It didn't matter. They hated me. And I think they hated Mal as a result. She was just trying to help me get my shit together, but they didn't care. They put her through hell.

I had some anger issues early on that put a strain on our relationship. Mal told me she wasn't sure if I was the one. We were at North Avenue Beach one day. I was obsessed with the beach. I was being a chatterbox, like always, and Mal was kind of off. I could tell something was bothering her. I asked if she wanted to talk about anything, and she told me I might not be the one. She said she didn't think we should talk about marriage or kids anymore, because she wasn't sure if it was in the cards for us. That was a wake-up call for me. I had not come this far to lose it all. I would have nothing. I couldn't lose her. I decided from that point on, I was going to fight for her every single day of my life. I have always fought for her since. And I always will. It might not always come out the right way. If you know me, you know I can be stubborn and hardheaded. But I've never loved someone this much. I would do anything for her.

After Mal's lease was up with her mean roommates, I finally got the hell out of Nick's house, and we got our own apartment in

Edgewater, right by the lake. After about a year, we decided we were ready to move to California, where Mal is from. Well, I had been ready from day one, but Mal had wanted to enjoy Chicago a bit longer. She got a really great job at a cool company in Los Angeles and wanted me to go with her. So I did. When Mal got that job, and they offered to pay to move us to California, I felt like we were the luckiest people in the world.

I had a job lined up as a security guard at a mall in LA, but that didn't work out. I worked retail for a while. I was really good at it. I could sell anything to anyone. But they cut my hours back to something like four hours a week, so I knew it wouldn't work long-term. I didn't have a future there. I delivered food on the side to make extra money. Then Mal's company had an opening for a customer support representative, so I applied. I figured it couldn't be any worse than what I was doing. I got the job, but I wasn't very good at it. If we're being totally honest, that job wasn't for me. People would call in and yell at me because they wanted their seventy-five cents back, and I just didn't care. I sat in our tiny studio apartment all day while people called me the N-word because I couldn't give them a refund. It was not fun. They ended up moving the customer support team to another state, so I was going to be out of a job if I didn't find something else. I applied for a different role in the company, on a different team. I got the job and have been part of the team ever since, all thanks to Mal. She encouraged me and helped me the entire way. We have nonstop fun. Our journey together has been the most fulfilling thing. It's been lifesaving for me. We've had a lot of highlights. Our wedding was obviously one of those—the first look, the pictures, the party. Best day ever. I felt like I won the championship that day.

Mal changed my life in so many ways. When we met, I didn't know how to take care of myself. It sounds silly, but one of the first things she did to change my life was teach me how to shop for pants. I didn't have any good pants. All my jeans were huge and baggy and didn't fit. I didn't know any better. But Mal took me to Macy's and taught me how to shop and how my clothes should fit. She helped me learn how to be a human being. She taught me how to grow up and be a responsible adult. I'd never had to pay my own bills or find my own apartment. Mal helped me learn things like that. When we met, I was posting inappropriate things on social media—violent shit, song lyrics about suicide, and so on. People didn't always know they were song lyrics, so Mal's friends would see my status updates and reach out, all concerned, because they thought I was going to kill myself. Mal helped me with that. She helped me understand why that wasn't appropriate and how I could deal with those feelings off of social media. She also helped me with my anger. One day, she told me I had to go to therapy, or she would leave. She was not putting up with my crap anymore. So I went to therapy. My therapist, Katie, helped me so much. She helped me understand why I was angry, where Mal was coming from when we argued, and the negative impacts of my anger on our relationship. Katie saved me. It was hard at first, but therapy helped me keep Mal in my life and be better for her. Counseling changed my life. It prevented me from killing myself, honestly.

Mal has been along on this journey for every bump in the road, every complaint, every story, every time I've said something mean about anyone. There were times I'd get in the car and have insane road rage and just start cursing people out. And she sat there for every incident and made me feel better every time. She'd give insight about the situation, tell me the best course of action, and teach me lessons about how to improve. I mean, she's basically been my Bat Computer for the past eight years. There were days I came home and wanted to quit, but she picked me up off the floor every time, without fail. Every time, she got me up, dusted me off, and told me I was okay. She always tells me to hang in there and not give up. And I listen. I don't listen to anybody, but I listen to her. I respect her so much. She's the best teammate I could ever ask for.

I'm forever bonded to Mal. You can't replace what we have. Other people might look prettier on the surface or have more money than us, but underneath all that, some of those people are monsters. What we have is forever. I was fortunate enough to get somebody who fits me like a puzzle piece. I don't even know where I would be without her. I don't think I would be here. At some point of every day, I choke up because I am so honored to be with her. It's such a privilege. To have someone who cares about me as much as she does is really special. When we first met, I was in shambles. Mallory picked up the pieces and put me back together.

The biggest thing of all was that Mal never judged me. Her mom criticized me. Her friends criticized me. I was rough around the edges, and I didn't have a college degree. That matters to some people. But none of it mattered to Mal. She always hung in. She could hang tough no matter the odds and just stick in there. She's efficient, smart, and beautiful, and her mind is fucking amazing. I've never met a more beautiful mind, honestly, even with her quirks or silly decorating projects. I really don't have an interest in how she arranges the silverware drawer, but for her I'll pretend to. I know it makes her happy. And all I want in this life is to make her happy. I'm forever grateful for everything she's done for me, and I wouldn't be in the position I'm in today without her.

Without Mal, I didn't stand a chance. She's been there for me for all the highs and the lows. She shows up every day. It doesn't matter if I'm happy or sad or angry. She's always here. She didn't sign up for my anger, but she never complains about it. She helps me through it. Mal always shows up for me. It doesn't matter what she's doing or what time of day it is. I've had issues in the middle of the night. She'll wake up, and she won't even be upset. It's just "what can I do? how can I help?" One time we had a tough argument, and I was thinking of ending my life, and she looked at me and said, "I just want you to be happy." And I knew she was telling the truth. No matter what I said or did, she would always have my back. She'd tell me exactly what I needed to hear, and I'd respond with "Fuck that!" but then she would bring me back to reality. And I'd listen. And it would work. I'm telling you, without this person in my life, I'm nothing. There are no words to tell her how much she means to me. She's unbelievable, always so positive and cheerful, like a little angel. A little bouncy angel. My angel.

About the Author

ORIGINALLY FROM UPSTATE NEW YORK, LAZARUS (NOW CHRIS) lives in Los Angeles with his wife Mallory and their cat Nala. This is Chris's first book.

Lightning Source UK Ltd.
Milton Keynes UK
UKHW012318301120
374401UK00006B/282/J